Photographer's LEGAL Guide

by

Carolyn E. Wright, Esq.

First Edition

Law Office of Carolyn E. Wright, LLC, Decatur, Georgia

Published by:
Law Office of Carolyn E. Wright, LLC
2107 N. Decatur Rd. #117
Decatur, GA 30033

Updates to the *Photographer's Legal Guide* are available at www.photoattorney.com

ISBN# 0-9790353-0-9

Printed in the United States of America

Disclaimer:

The information provided in this book is for educational purposes only and does not purport to constitute legal advice. The author and publisher make no warranty, express or implied, including the warranties of merchantability and fitness for a particular purpose. The author and publisher do not assume any legal liability or responsibility for the accuracy, completeness, or usefulness of any information, product, or process disclosed, and do not represent that its use would not infringe on privately-owned rights. Use this book at your own risk.

All company names, product names, service marks, and trademarks referred to in this book are the property of their respective owners. Unless otherwise noted, Carolyn E. Wright and The Law Office of Carolyn E. Wright, LLC, are not affiliated with any of the trademark or service mark holders or vendors referenced herein. Use of a trademark or service mark or any other term in this book should not be regarded as affecting the validity of the mark.

Dedication

This book is dedicated to photographers who catch the wonders of the world one shutter at a time.

Table of Contents

Foreword

For the past 24 years, photographing birds has been the driving passion in my life. When I am in the field striving to create beautiful images of free and wild birds, I never think of the possibility of selling this or that photograph. And I never photograph with specific markets in mind. And I certainly don't think about registering my copyrights . . . . Photography has evolved dramatically in the past few years, and with digital capture taking the world by storm, many do not realize that with all of its wonderful advantages, digital has made it easier for folks to grab our images for their own use. After reading Carolyn Wright's "Photographer's Legal Guide" I realized that I have been living—and working—in the dark. When it comes to registering my copyrights and pursuing infringers, I have lots of catching up to do, and with Carolyn's guide in hand, my job will be a lot easier, and better yet, my work will be fully protected.

As I read through several drafts of this work, I was amazed to learn how much I did not know. And I learned that much of what I thought I knew about photography and the law was simply wrong. Lots of folks are free with legal advice, and much of the "information" passed along is—though well-intentioned—erroneous. Misconceptions abound, but having the Legal Guide in hand is like having a top-notch lawyer on retainer.

"You do not need to register your copyright in order to sue for infringement." "You can use that music with your slide program without any problem." "The copyright registered by the book or magazine publisher who used your images will fully protect your rights." "That statue is on government property, everyone knows that you can photograph it with impunity." "A handshake is as good and legally binding as having a signed usage agreement in place." Which of the above statements are true? How many of them have you heard? I had heard them repeated so many times that I assumed that they were all true, but in the Legal Guide, I learned that each is incorrect . . . .

I first met Carolyn Wright when she attended my "The Art of Nature Photography: It Ain't Just Birds!" weekend seminars in Atlanta, GA. It was there that I learned about www.photoattorney.com. Her website was and is chock full of helpful legal information for all photographers, not just folks who enjoy making images of their favorite natural history subjects. I was so impressed with the "photo attorney" that I began calling her often for legal advice.

I have come to know Carolyn as a smart, pleasant, helpful, and ethical attorney, who cares about photography and photographers. In addition to her legal expertise, Carolyn is a professional photographer who teaches and writes on the subject. As a result, she understands the legal issues that are unique to our profession. Her writing is clear and concise; she has the ability to make even the most complex legal statute make sense, even to a legal dummy like me . . . .

As someone who would rather be thinking about the direction and quality of the light than how the legal ramifications of my death will affect my images, their copyrights, and my heirs, the "Photographer's Legal Guide" is a most welcome addition to my library.   And like any good photography book, it is one to be studied often. Learning the material well and following Carolyn's step by step instructions will help all photographers become proficient at registering their copyrights promptly and correctly and protecting the images that they devote so much time and energy to create.

Best and love and great picture-making to all,

artie

Note: Arthur Morris has been a Canon contract photographer since 1994 and continues in that role today.

Introduction

PhotoAttorney was born from my love and support of the arts. I begged my mother for piano lessons at age 10 and started snapping pictures at age 12 when my father gave me my first SLR. My path in the arts began early and culminated with a degree in music and a professional photography business.

It became clear that understanding the law is an essential component to protecting art. From my desire to help others defend their work, I went to law school and directed my studies towards those areas that affect artists—copyright, trademark, contract, and entertainment law.

After ten years of general law practice representing Fortune 100 companies in multi-million dollar litigations, I turned my attention to the law as it affects photographers. The law shapes photographers' lives differently than it does other artists. But little was being done to help photographers understand those nuances.

The PhotoAttorney blog began in 2005 as a legal education resource for photographers. The response was overwhelming. Photographers were excited about a reliable source of information rather than turning to the rumor mill that is full of inaccuracies and myths. This book expands on that process to provide an organized foundation of information.

The *Photographer's Legal Guide* is not designed as a comprehensive legal analysis full of case citations and statutory sections. Instead, my job is to give you the essential tools and basic information to help you protect your work while not putting you to sleep. Your job is to use that information to know what do to, how to do it, or when to get professional help so that you can spend more time taking beautiful photographs.

Here's to each of our creative endeavors.

Take my advice; get professional help.
PhotoAttorney

Acknowledgements

Thanks to my mother who gave me a creative eye and provides continuous love and support.

Thanks to my father who first taught me photography and challenged me to do my best.

Thanks to Artie Morris who provided significant editorial contributions and assistance. Thanks to Linda East Robbins for her editorial revisions.

Thanks to Jennifer Dandy for her editorial suggestions and proofreading.

Thanks to Bob Keller for his love, guidance, and encouragement.

How To Use This Book

This book is designed to help photographers understand essential legal principles so that they can protect their work. Generally based on the law in the United States, it is not intended to replace personalized legal and business advice. State laws can vary, situations are different, and needs fluctuate so that it is impossible to provide specific advice on a given circumstance in advance. But once the photographer knows generally the issues presented in business and law, the photographer will be alerted to those areas that need professional assistance.

Take my advice; get professional help.
PhotoAttorney

                                                              Photographer's Legal Guide

Getting Started With Your Photography Business

Types of Businesses

Some photographers are satisfied with their photography as a hobby. Others choose to operate it as a side business to earn some money from it. A few turn their photography business into full-time careers.

If you decide to start a full- or part-time photography business, you'll need to select what kind of business it's going to be. There are several types of legal entities to choose from, with financial and operational pros and cons for each of them. Evaluate the options carefully and seek advice from an attorney and an accountant before making the decision. You can later change your form of business, but that can be difficult and may require extensive documentation.

The types of business entities and some of their advantages and disadvantages follow.

Sole Proprietorship

A sole proprietorship is a one-person shop. It doesn't include relatives, business partners, or friends. In some states, it includes your spouse. It's you alone. One advantage of a sole proprietorship is that it's easy to set up—you can establish yourself as a business by simply declaring it. That is, you can state, "I am starting my 'ABC Photography' business today." It's helpful to document it in some way, such as opening a bank account or starting a general ledger in your accounting software. Note the date that you begin your business, too. You may need to be officially registered with your county or state (see "Business Licenses" below). You also may need to register your "fictitious name" [also known as a trade name, doing business as, or DBA] such as "PhotoAttorney" with your state or county government if your operate your business under a name other than your legal name. But you have to do little else to be recognized as a sole proprietorship.

The income or loss from your business is included on your personal tax return, so you are only taxed once. You file a Schedule C to record the business's income and expenses. You probably can complete Schedule C without professional assistance. You may want to take some courses with the Small Business Administration or the IRS to learn basic accounting and tax skills. There also are good software packages to help you keep up with your business records. Check the Appendix for a list.

If you sell even one print to someone else, you should report the income to the IRS. If you don't consider yourself to have a business in photography, then it is a hobby where the deductible expenses are limited to the income from the hobby.

See more about this in the chapter on Running Your Photography Business—Tax Advantages for the Photographer.

As a sole proprietor, there is no legal separation between you and the photography business. So if someone sues your business, the complaining party can get not only to your photography property, but also to your personal assets. Your creditors also can seize your personal accounts. Be sure to maintain adequate insurance that covers both your personal and company property. It also can be difficult to show that you are a legitimate business if you are a sole proprietor, and you may have difficulty getting loans or credit.

As a sole proprietor, you generally use your social security number to identify the business. That makes your SSN more susceptible to theft and makes it easier for creditors to access your personal assets. Even as sole proprietor, you may get a tax identification number (see "Tax ID Number" below) to identify your business.

As your business grows, you may want to change your form of business to another type. It is easy to convert to another business structure, but is more difficult to transfer back to a sole proprietorship. If you are not sure how large your business will grow, the sole proprietorship is a good beginning option.

Partnerships

Another kind of business entity is the partnership, and it can be in the form of a general or limited partnership. A general partnership is similar to the sole proprietorship, but you share the business equally with one or more partners. You can pool your assets so that you appear to be a stronger entity. Partners do not have to contribute the same items, amount, or work to the partnership. Your personal assets, along with the personal assets of the partners, are still vulnerable to creditors and judgment holders. Your exposure to liability is increased because one partner can be responsible for the entire debts and actions of the partnership. Like the sole proprietorship, the tax obligations of the partnership pass through to the individuals and are thus taxed only once.

It helps, but it is not required, to have a written partnership agreement so that each partner knows what is expected from the partnership. You may want to get an attorney to help you draft the partnership agreement because the attorney can anticipate issues you may not think about. Unless specified otherwise, there are general rules for a partnership that a court will imply and enforce. Some of these rules mandate that: (1) each partner has an equal vote in the decisions of the partnership; (2) new members cannot join the partnership unless all partners agree; and (3) partners must share equally in the profits and losses of the partnership. In addition, a simple majority vote is needed for ordinary decisions in the partnership, but a unanimous vote is required to change fundamental characters of the partnership. The partnership can be terminated by any partner. You will need a partnership agreement in place if you want to change these general rules.

General partnerships usually do not require any formal organizational meeting or state filing to begin the partnership. You begin them as you do a sole proprietor-

                          Photographer's Legal Guide

ship. However, the partnership must fulfill all obligations required of businesses such as business licenses, trade name registration, or permits.

A limited partnership is a combination of a general partnership and a corporation. A limited partner may fund the partnership but not be exposed to liabilities of the partnership. A limited partnership has to have one or more general partners who are responsible for the day-to-day operations of the business. The general partner is subject to personal liability, just as in the general partnership. The limited partner (or partners—there can be many), however, is vulnerable only to the amount given to the partnership. A limited partnership must be registered with your state government office, and the partners with their designations are identified in the filing. This form of business is ideal when you have an investor who is not interested in running the business but would like to share in the profits. It also limits the general partner's liability because he has no obligation to repay the limited partners if there are no profits.

A limited liability partnership (LLP) is a relatively new and unique type of limited partnership allowed in some states. The LLP provides for limited liability of all partners, even if they are involved in the management of the business. It was created for those businesses that previously were not allowed to incorporate, such as law firms. Check with your Secretary of State's office to determine whether the LLP is allowed in your state and its requirements.

Corporations

Corporations are business entities separate from those who own them. Their liability is limited to their assets. As long as the corporation is treated as a separate entity, creditors and judgment holders cannot get to the personal assets of the stockholders. Instead, only the property that belongs to the corporation is potentially exposed to liabilities.

Corporations are made up of three parties—shareholders, directors, and officers. In small corporations, a person may fill two or even all three of these roles. The shareholders own the corporation and elect the directors. The directors oversee the general affairs of the corporation and appoint the officers. The officers direct the day-to-day business operations of the corporation.

The major disadvantage to running a corporation is the amount of legal and tax documents that are required to establish and maintain it. Also, because corporations file separate tax returns, profits are subject to double taxation when they are distributed to shareholders. A stockholder may be personally liable for wrongful acts that go beyond the mission of the corporation, such as creating a defamatory work or stealing a copyright for a photography business.

You must respect the separateness of the corporation for it to remain intact. For example, you cannot mix your personal and corporate money and assets. Likewise, a client hires the corporation—not you—to photograph an event. If you continue to operate as a photographer separate from the business rather than as an employee of the photography company, a creditor can "pierce the veil" of your corporation and claim your personal assets.

Changing your business from a sole proprietorship or partnership to a corporation is relatively easy. If you have significant personal assets you want to protect, or when you begin to hire employees rather than contractors, you may want to consider incorporating your business.

There are two types of corporations for tax purposes: a subchapter "C" corporation and a subchapter "S" corporation. The Sub-S Corporation has stricter operational requirements, but the profit or loss passes through to your personal income so it is not subjected to double taxation, as is a C-corporation.

While stockholders can buy shares of a company, you should be careful about how you take funds from outside investors so that you don't violate Securities and Exchange Commission laws. You cannot sell unregistered securities/stock. Get advice from a lawyer to set this up correctly.

Limited Liability Company

A limited liability company (LLC) is a relatively new form of business entity allowed in some states. It combines some of the advantages of a partnership with some of the advantages of a corporation. Recently, states have allowed one-person LLCs. "Members" of LLCs are protected from personal liability. IRS regulations provide that LLCs with more than one member will be taxed as a partnership unless it elects to be taxed as a corporation. If taxed as a partnership, the earnings will be apportioned to the members and then taxed at their personal tax rates. LLCs with only one member will be taxed as a sole proprietorship.

The personal liability of an LLC's member is limited to the assets of the LLC, except in the event of wrongful acts such as those noted above in the corporation section. Any of the members can manage the company or designate others (regardless of whether that person is a member) to do so. Ownership of the LLC is easily transferred to another. The requirements for setting up an LLC are similar but less stringent compared to the requirements for establishing a corporation. While you may need legal and accounting assistance to start and maintain an LLC, it is an attractive business form that a photographer should consider.

Fictitious Names, Trade Names, or "Doing Business As" (DBA)

As a sole proprietorship, you may need to register your "fictitious name" (also known as a trade name, doing business as, or DBA) with your state or county government if you operate your business under a name other than your legal name. As an LLC or corporation, you may use fictitious names to operate multiple businesses without creating separate legal entities for each one. For example, you may run a portrait business (DBA "Heartfelt Photos") and a photo workshop company (DBA "Vivid Wildlife Workshops") as part of the same LLC.

Maintaining the Protection of a Business Entity

The corporation and limited liability company create a "corporate veil" between your personal and business assets to provide personal liability protection against lawsuits, creditors, and other disputes. But if you don't honor the formalities of the business, you can lose those advantages.

Unlike a proprietorship or a partnership, a corporation or company is a legal entity separate and distinct from you as an individual. When you establish the corporation or company you must do more than register it with the state. You also must follow a host of ongoing legal requirements to prove that you have a bona fide business entity instead of a sham created to dodge personal liability. Otherwise, your opponents will be able to "pierce the corporate veil" to set aside the corporation and then use your personal assets to satisfy the business' obligations.

Here are ten ways to maintain the protection of a business entity:

- Follow all state and federal requirements by filing annual registrations and by holding annual meetings and taking minutes. (Additional information is available from your Secretary of State—search on the internet for your state's name and the words "secretary of state"—and the IRS at www.irs. gov);

- Keep personal and company assets separated in different bank accounts;

- Set up the corporation so that it is not dependent on assets that it does not own or control;

- Don't conduct business that may constitute a conflict of interest;

- Use your company name rather than your name on all marketing and business materials;

- Treat yourself as an employee of the company and the company as a separate and different entity;

- Sign your business materials as the employee, not as yourself. It would be correct to sign "Carolyn E. Wright, President, Law Office of Carolyn E. Wright, LLC";

- Avoid corporate debt when the business is insolvent;

- Don't use the business assets to benefit you personally;

·   Conduct your business within the scope of the incorporation or company documents (i.e.; don't provide plumbing services as part of the photography business).

Forming a corporation or company for your photography business is only the first step towards protecting your personal assets. Treat and operate your business as a business so that your customers and creditors will, too.

Tax ID Number

Once you establish your business, you may need an employer identification number (EIN), also known as a federal tax identification number. It is a nine-digit number that the IRS assigns to business entities to identify taxpayers who are required to file various business tax returns. EINs are used by employers, sole proprietors, corporations, partnerships, non-profit organizations, and other business entities. You need to get one if you operate your business as a corporation or a partnership, have employees, have a Keogh plan, or have other specific tax needs. Talk with your accountant or check with your state to determine whether you need a separate state number or charter.

Even if you don't fit into any of these categories, a tax ID number can be helpful when getting bank accounts, when getting paid by corporations, or when dealing with other businesses. It gives your photography extra clout by appearing to validate your business.

You apply for your EIN using Form SS-4. You may: call the Business and Specialty Tax Line at (800) 829-4933 from 7:00 a.m. to 10:00 p.m., Monday through Friday; apply online at https://sa.www4.irs.gov/sa_vign/newFormSS4.do; or apply by fax or mail.

Business Licenses

Depending on where you live, your local and state governments may require that you get a license to conduct your business. This is especially true when you are operating a business under a name other than your own (see requirements for operating under a fictitious name above). You may need one or more licenses, perhaps a state license and another from your city. Check with your local Chamber of Commerce, Secretary of State and/or the city and state treasurers to determine their licensing requirements. In most states, you can do this research online. Be aware that failure to secure these licenses can result in costly penalties.

Having a business license is not only about paying fees to your municipality. It can be a business advantage as well. Once you get the licenses, display them to your clients. It will show them that you are serious about your business. You may also be included on business lists compiled by your local Chamber of Commerce that will help your marketing efforts.

You can more easily collect sales tax if you have a business license. If you buy products for resale, having a license can save you money because you can buy equipment that will be exempt from sales tax. Some vendors won't sell to you or give you discounts without a business license. Banks may require a business license to open a checking account or merchant's account so that you can accept payment by credit cards.

Zoning Laws

Many photographers run their business from home, especially when they first start. While you have the right to photograph on your property, certain activities may violate business and zoning laws for your neighborhood or city. Your subdivision also may have covenants restricting you from running a business out of your home. If you are thinking about buying a house, check the records in the county's office to see whether restrictive covenants are on file or ask the real estate agent/home owner for a copy of them. You also must be careful that your activities do not encroach unfairly on your neighbors' rights. While it will be hard for your neighbors to stop you from photography activities they aren't aware of, it can become an issue if many clients frequent your home office/portrait studio causing traffic and parking problems.

Trademarks/Servicemarks for Your Business

Trademarks or servicemarks allow people to identify the source of goods or services, not the products or services themselves. When people see your trademark, they will know where the product came from or who is providing the service. Trademarks can be names, symbols, packaging, the shape of a product, the colors of a product, the sounds, or scents associated with the product, or any combination of these. If a customer can identify the source of a product or service based on the trademark, then you have developed "secondary meaning" and have a strong trademark. To promote, protect, and keep your business from being confused with another, you should consider establishing a trademark for your business. Once you obtain a trademark, you should vigorously defend it. Then, no one in your line of business can use your trademark.

A trademark cannot be a generic name, such as "photography." It's harder to get the rights to a trademark that is merely descriptive, referencing a component of the product, such as "portrait photography." But if you can demonstrate secondary meaning for the mark, then you get registration rights for it. The next level of a trademark is a suggestive mark that requires a "leap of imagination," such as "Portrayals."

An arbitrary trademark is an existing word that has no relation to the goods or service, such as "Silver Photography" (as long as you are not selling pictures of silver and silver is not your name). Fanciful marks are coined terms with no prior meaning, made up for use as a trademark, such as "Kixxy Photography."

Rights to use a trademark come from using the mark in commerce with the product or service. You may use the TM symbol immediately with your trademark, but you may only use the ® symbol after federally registering the trademark.

A trademark can be registered at both the state and federal levels. Since the Internet allows photographers to reach clients beyond their locality, registering at both levels gives you the best protection. But if you plan to keep your business at the state level, you need only to register there.

Before you begin the registration process, you should check first to see if someone else is using the same or a similar mark. You can do this by searching the Internet, the Yellow Pages, your state's trademark registry and the federal registry. If you find no competing or similar marks, you may use your mark in business and should register it as soon as possible. You can register your mark in several ways—the plain words/numbers that make up the mark, the way the words are presented, and the way your product is packaged. All of these must be distinctive and will be intensely scrutinized by the United States Patent and Trademark Office ("PTO") so that others are not unfairly prevented from using these marks. After an investigative period, the Office may grant or reject your trademark.

If you find a similar mark during your search, you may want to revise your trademark/business name. Even if the other business' trademark is not registered, if it has been in use for a long time and has achieved what is known as "secondary meaning," you may be prevented from using your trademark in certain areas and for certain purposes.

At the national level, the PTO offers two federal trademark registers—the Principal Register and the Supplemental Register. Marks may be registered on the Principal Register if they are shown to distinguish the applicant's goods and services. Marks may be registered on the Supplemental Register if they pass the more moderate test of being "capable of distinguishing applicant's goods or services."

Registration on either the Principal or Supplemental Registers:

> · allows the owner of the registered mark to use the registration symbol ® to deter infringers and impress customers;

> · provides protection under §39(b) of the Lanham Act against state restrictions on use of the mark;

> · gives priority rights in registering in foreign countries according to the provisions of international treaties; and

> · places the mark on the PTO database and website at http://www.uspto.gov to serve as notice and may prevent others from adopting the same or similar mark.

Registration on the Principal Register provides the following additional advantages:

- provides constructive notice to those who might later adopt the mark;

- is prima facie evidence of the mark's validity and registration as well as evidence of the registrant's ownership and exclusive right to use the mark in commerce;

- allows the mark owner the right to ex parte seizure of goods bearing a counterfeit mark ("a spurious mark that is identical with, or substantially indistinguishable from, a registered mark");

- gives the owner the right to treble damages (a multiple of actual damages) and attorneys' fees against intentional use of a counterfeit mark, in the absence of extenuating circumstances;

- provides a deterrent effect of severe criminal penalties for the use of counterfeit marks;

- allows the owner to have the Bureau of Customs exclude imports bearing infringing marks; and

- gives the owner the right to apply to have the mark declared "incontestable" (although it can still be challenged, it is the highest form of protection available) after five years on the Principal Register and compliance with certain formalities.

Registration of the mark on the Supplemental Register, while not providing the more expansive protection of a mark registered on the Principal Register, will provide the following benefits to the registrant:

- allows the owner to file an infringement action in federal court;

- gives the PTO the ability to cite the mark against a later application by a third party for a substantially similar mark on the Principal Register;

- provides the owner the opportunity to have the mark registered on the Principal Register. This can be accomplished by showing that the mark has acquired "secondary meaning." A showing of secondary meaning may be demonstrated once the mark has been in use for a period of time, usually five years.

You always have the right to use your own name for your business regardless of whether it has been trademarked by someone else. However, marks that are primarily surnames will not be given protection by the Trademark Office. The down side to using your name for your business is the difficulty in selling that business.

Many states also require you to file a fictitious name or trade name statement when you operate a business under a different name, such as a trademark. See the requirements for operating under a fictitious name above.

Domain/Website Names

Owning a domain name for a website or registering your business name with your state or local government is not the same as registering your trademark. Likewise, having a trademark does not ensure that you can obtain the same domain name. You must secure each of those separately. However, to support your trademarks or service marks, you may want to register all related domain names for your marks. That will keep "cybersquatters" from trading on or diluting your trademark. For example, I registered "photoattorney.com" along with "photoattorney.net," "photoattorney.org," "photoattorney.biz."

Be sure to not let your registrations lapse. If someone else registers a domain name similar to yours, you may wait for the expiration of the name (you can backorder the domain name at www.snapnames.com or www.godaddy.com), buy it outright from the person who owns it, arbitrate under ICAAN's Uniform Dispute Resolution Policy, or sue under the Anti-Cybersquatting Consumer Protection Act.

Running Your Photography Business

Marketing Your Products and Services

When photographers start their businesses, they often think that expensive equipment and photo technique are most important. Seasoned professional photographers know, however, that running your photography as a business is vital to its sustainability. Running your business well includes marketing your services, understanding legal issues, and keeping good accounting and tax records.

When you market your products and services, be aware of the legal restrictions on your activities. While it is important to promote your work, you want to keep your marketing lawful and ethical. Following are some important factors to guide you when publicizing your services:

- Whenever you market your photography business, it must be truthful and not misleading. It's acceptable to use salesmanship and to boast about your work. The legal term for this is called "puffery." But you should not be deceitful in your promotions.

- Don't engage in "bait and switch" tactics by advertising one product that isn't available and then trying to sell a different, more expensive product to a customer who responds to your ad. Don't advertise products you can't deliver.

- Advertising on any website, whether it's on your own or another website, should be treated the same as any other advertising. Any ad that would be illegal on the radio, on television, or in print generally would be illegal on the web. You must follow those laws for all forms of media—the web is not excluded.

Regulations for Commercial Email

Photographers often use email for marketing purposes. But emails that primarily are intended to advertise or promote a commercial product or service are subject to federal legislation referred to as "CAN-SPAM." The Act establishes specific requirements for those commercial emails, so it's important to be aware of the provisions.

There are four basic requirements of the Act:

- You may not have false or misleading header information— your "to," "from" and routing information must be accurate.

- You may not have a deceptive subject line—your "subject line" cannot mislead the recipient.

- You must give the recipient a way to opt out of further mailings—such as an email address to send a request for removal.

- Your email must be designated as an advertisement and it must include your physical mailing address.

A "transactional" or "relationship" message—an email regarding an agreed-upon transaction or one that updates your relationship with an existing customer—is not subject to the CAN-SPAM provisions except that it may not contain false or misleading routing information. Other types of emails are exempt from the CAN-SPAM Act.

Violating these provisions may result in fines of up to $11,000. Nevertheless, the requirements of the Act are good business practices to follow, regardless of your email's purpose.

Pricing Your Products and Services

Setting a price for your products and services is more than just finding a happy medium between one that's so high that you lose customers or so low that you're giving away the farm. You also must consider some legal factors when setting your prices. The safest way to establish your fees is to have a reasonable and consistent basis for what you charge. Here are pricing tips to help you get started:

- The prices you advertise are the prices you must charge. You may have exclusions for your pricing, such as "prices are subject to change," but the price you advertise for one is the price you must charge for all.

- Offer your goods and services at the same price without respect to your clients' race, religion, sexual orientation, etc.

- Do not engage in price gouging or other deceptive pricing practices. In other words, you must have some basis for the price you set. Check with your attorney and state laws for specifics, but essentially your pricing must be reasonable.

- Don't charge some clients one fee and other clients a different fee for the same photographic services.

- Check with your state authorities to determine the maximum interest and penalties that you can charge for extending credit.

- Some resources to determine what others are charging are the Stock Photo Price Calculator at http://photographers-index.com/stockprice.htm, www.fotoquote.com, and www.hindsightltd.com/products/PriceGuide.html.

- You may research what other photographers charge for products and services but avoid antitrust activity by not telling other photographers what to charge. Don't make agreements with other photographers to fix your prices.

- Don't run promotions offering to pay sales taxes on goods without clearing it with the Federal Trade Commission and your state authorities.

- Don't advertise products and services that you can't deliver.

Setting your prices can be tricky. If you're fair about it, you'll get all the business you can handle.

Resale of Products

Many photographers resell products such as photo albums, frames, or even photographic accessories. To do this, you need to be licensed to sell these products by getting permission from, and often by signing a contract with, the manufacturer or distributor. If you advertise these products, you may be bound by "Minimum Advertised Price" agreements. The specifics will be included in the contract with the manufacturer. Follow them exactly.

Gift Certificates

Offering gift certificates for portrait sessions, prints, and other products and services can add to your business. To protect yourself, include certain items in your certificates. Be sure they have a date of issue, an expiration date, your signature, and a statement that says the gift certificate has no cash value.

Selling on Consignment or Leasing Your Photographs

Photographers often lease artwork to businesses or sell photos on consignment. But if the business or gallery goes bankrupt, your photos may become part of the bankruptcy estate. The creditors of the business or gallery then may seize your work without further obligation to you.

Some states have enacted laws to protect photographers in these specific instances. For example, the Uniform Commercial Code ["UCC"] has been enacted in some form in every state. Check with your local attorney to determine whether your state has adopted the specific UCC provisions that will protect your consigned goods from being seized. The UCC in general affords three ways to shelter your consigned work:

- File a UCC-1 form (also known as UCC Form 1) at the time of the consignment in the county where gallery is located.

- Have the gallery owner post a sign telling the public that the goods are consigned (this option is not available in all states).

- Prove that creditors were aware that the gallery sold consigned goods.

The UCC Form 1 makes you a secured creditor for the gallery, giving you a legal claim for your photographs. It's essentially the same thing as a mortgage on your house. Be sure to remove the lien when the photograph is sold. The last two provisions are more difficult to enforce, but are becoming more commonplace.

Other states have passed laws purposely to protect consigned goods. Many of them require the consignment agreement to be in writing. Following are some necessary and other helpful items to include in the agreement:

- who is responsible for damage to the photographs

- prices to charge for the photographs

- specific list and description of the photographs being consigned

- the gallery's fees and responsibilities

- the requirement that the gallery post a sign that the goods are consigned

It also may help to include a clause in the consignment contract that states: "If any lien, attachment or bankruptcy petition is placed against the Gallery, this Agreement shall terminate immediately and the Gallery will return all of the Photographer's works to the Photographer." If the gallery files bankruptcy or becomes insolvent, get a lawyer to help you protect your property.

Get Professional Accounting Help

Once you create a business for your photography, you must maintain complete and accurate records of your revenue and expenses. You will have federal and state reporting requirements as well as some obligation to pay taxes. You may spend the time learning the accounting and tax rules yourself and hope that you get them right or you may hire a certified public accountant ("CPA") to do it properly in a shorter amount of time. Following are some of the important tax and accounting concerns for photographers.

Sales Tax

Many photographers sell their work either on the side or as a full-time job. Those sales may be subject to sales tax. Since the photographer, as the seller, is responsible for collecting and paying those taxes, you should understand your tax obligations to protect your business.

Sales taxes are imposed by state and local governments including counties and cities, but each state handles them differently. For example, some states don't require tax collection for services, only for goods. California photographers who deliver images electronically do not have to collect sales tax from their clients. In some other states, you must collect sales tax for all photography services, including materials, services, and fees.

Tax obligations may apply only if you sell your work on a retail basis (direct to the public) rather than wholesale (to a middle person). For example, if you sell your prints directly to individuals, you need to charge sales tax. If a gallery sells your prints, the gallery is responsible for collecting and remitting sales tax.

You should separate the sales tax amount from your charges on your invoice or receipt or state specifically that the total due includes sales tax. In the latter case, you must remit the collected tax by backing it out of the total amount received.

If you sell products or services to someone who lives in another state, you may not have to collect sales tax for that transaction. However, a few states, such as Texas, require that you pay sales tax for sales to persons in that state regardless of your location.

How do you determine your tax obligations? Consult your state treasurer's office, a tax attorney or an accountant. Even then, you may get different information than your colleague receives. So get the advice in writing. You may be relieved of tax, penalty, and interest charges that are due on a transaction if the state's treasurer determines that you reasonably relied on written advice that was erroneous and were harmed by that reliance.

It's important to understand your tax liabilities. If you do not collect and remit the correct amount, you may owe the taxes due plus penalties and interest. They can mount quickly.

Tax Advantages for Your Photography

Regardless of whether your photography is a business or a hobby, you can use it to make a difference in your tax obligation. Specifically, if you are running a photography business, even part-time, the costs to run it can offset your income—not just the income from your photography business but from your day job, as well. If your photography is a hobby, then the costs to support it can be deducted from the income from your photography. Because the tax code changes every year, you or your accountant must keep apprised of those expenses that can be deducted.

Is Your Photography a Hobby or a Business?

To properly handle your deductions, you must first determine whether your photography is a hobby or a business. To be declared a business, your goal must be to make a profit. But since photography is expensive, it can take a long time to show a profit. So are you out of luck? Maybe not!

Here are some ways to demonstrate to the IRS that you are running a photography business:

- Make a profit in three out of five consecutive years, and you need to show nothing else.

- Keep accurate and updated business books and records on your activities.

- Leave your time-consuming day job or reduce your time there to devote to your business.

- Market and promote your business.

- Follow standard or develop routine practices for your business.

- Make attempts to reduce the disparity of your losses compared to your income from the business.

- Hire experts such as accountants, marketing firms and lawyers, or study ways to help your business make a profit.

- Experience losses similar to others in the same business.

- Operate your business like those who do make a profit with their photography business.

- Be able to show that your business will eventually make a profit.

Other than the first item, none of these will definitively prove that your photography activities are a business. Further, the IRS may look at many other factors to determine the purpose of your photography. Following the above practices will not only help to show that your photography is a business, it will actually help your business.

Tax Deductions for Photographers

Keeping good records is key to maximizing the tax advantages for both those who run a photography business or maintain it as a hobby. It also is important to understand what deductions are allowed and how to account for those expenses. Following are 10 tips for photographers to make the most of their tax advantages:

1. Record all income that you receive from your photography—every penny, every year. The IRS doesn't care if you miss a deduction or two, but it gets upset if you fail to report income.

2. Track your automobile expenses. You have two options here: you either can track the mileage you travel for photography purposes to deduct the government rate per mile ($0.445 for 2006); or you can calculate what it costs to operate your vehicle for the year and apply the percentage that you use your automobile for photography to determine your auto expense. For either method, record the starting mileage for your vehicle each year.

3. Travel expenses can be significant for photographers. The IRS publishes a per diem rate for standard expenses when on the road. Keep track of your photographic travel days for your photography if you choose that method, or track your actual "ordinary and necessary" travel expenses to deduct them. This includes transportation, such as travel by airplane, train, bus, or car between your home and your business destination, and taxi, commuter bus and airport limousine between the airport or station and your hotel, as well as from the hotel to your work location. Baggage and shipping expenses to send your materials or equipment to your destination are deductible. Your rental car expenses are deductible (only to the extent the car is used for business).

    If your business trip is overnight or long enough that you need to stop for sleep or rest to properly perform your duties, your lodging and meals are deductible. Meals include food, beverages, taxes and related tips, but they must not be "lavish or extravagant." You may deduct only 50% of the actual cost or of the standard meal allowance. The amount of the standard meal allowance is based on when and where you travel. For example, it was $31 a day for most locations in the United States from January through September of 2005. It jumped to $39 a day for the remainder of 2005. Most major cities and many other localities are designated as high-cost areas, qualifying for higher standard meal allowances. If you travel to more than one location in a day, use the rate for the place where you sleep or rest. For more information and current rates, review IRS publication 1542 or go to www.gsa.gov/perdiem. For rates for travel outside the continental United States, go to www.state.gov/m/a/als/prdm to determine the applicable rate to use.

You also may deduct dry cleaning and laundry expenses that are necessary while traveling. You may deduct the cost of business calls while on your business trip. Tips and other similar ordinary and necessary expenses are deductible, as well.

4. If you operate your photography business out of your home, you may deduct a percentage of your housing costs (mortgage, water, electricity, insurance, etc.) based on the proportion of the house that is used solely for photography. You may not deduct the expenses for both an office at home and elsewhere, such as at a studio.

5. You may deduct the cost of a phone line for your business as long as you also have a personal line. You also may deduct the cost of long distance calls made for your photography, so keep your phone records.

6. You may deduct the cost of photography seminars and workshops, so track those expenses.

7. You may allocate a proportion of your internet, website and computer expenses that support your photography business. Be sure to apportion an appropriate amount for your personal use, where applicable.

8. Keep receipts for all of your photography expenses including equipment, supplies and materials. Checks and credit card statements are helpful as proof of your costs, but they are not the preferred documentation.

9. Equipment that lasts more than one year (cameras, furniture, etc.) must be depreciated over the expected life of the item. You can deduct only a portion of its cost each year. Maintain a spreadsheet with the date of purchase and the depreciation schedule so that you will know the basis of the equipment if you sell it before the end of the five years. Be sure to check into the "section 179 deduction" that allows you to deduct the cost (up to a certain amount) of depreciable property in the year you buy it.

10. You may deduct your accountant and attorney fees (including fees for registering your copyrights) that support your photography business activities, so keep copies of invoices from those professionals.

ADDITIONAL RESOURCES

Additional information is available from IRS, especially in publications on specific topics. Those especially helpful to photographers include:

> Publication 463 Travel, Entertainment, Gift and Car Expenses
> Publication 552 Recordkeeping for Individuals
> Publication 525 Taxable and Non Taxable Income
> Publication 946 How To Depreciate Property
> Publication 529 Miscellaneous Deductions
> Publication 587 Business Use of Your Home
> Publication 1542 Per Diem Rates
> Publication 334 Tax Guide for Small Businesses
> Publication 917 Business Use of Your Car

You may download them at: http://www.irs.gov/formspubs/lists/0,,id=97819,00.html

Your New Year's resolutions should include keeping accurate records of your photography activities. Regardless of whether photography is a hobby or a business for you, understanding the implications of tax laws can help you make the most of your photography.

Donations to Charity

Many photographers are asked to donate prints or to license photographs to charitable organizations for use in their fundraising efforts. Is any of that deductible on your tax return? It depends.

IRS Publication 526 explains the rules related to charitable contributions. You can download a copy from the IRS website. It states that before you can deduct anything for such donations, you either have to itemize your deductions on a Schedule A (as opposed to taking the standard deduction) or you have to report the profit or loss from your photography business on a Schedule C or on your company's tax return. Your donation also must made be to a qualified organization (Publication 78 lists most qualified organizations or you can check the charitable organization's status with the IRS at 1-877-829-5500).

If you meet the above criteria, you may deduct the smaller amount of either the costs of the donated item (paper, ink, CD) or the fair market value of the property at the time of donation. The fair market value generally is the price at which the property would change hands between a willing buyer and a willing seller, neither having to buy or sell, and both having reasonable knowledge of all of the relevant facts.

In most cases, the costs of the donated print or photo will be less than the fair market value. For photographers who have an established photography business, they most likely have already deducted the costs (materials such as ink, paper and CDs) as business expenses and cannot again deduct the contribution. The hobbyist photographer who does not deduct photography materials for business purposes is the only one who really benefits from this situation.

What about your time and talent that it takes to take the photo? Publication 526 specifically states that you cannot deduct the value of your time or services.

You're also out of luck if you donate your entire copyright to a charity. IRS Form 8899 provides that you cannot deduct as intellectual property a copyright held by a taxpayer whose personal efforts created the property.

What can you do if you want to help the charity? Charge your normal fees for your work and otherwise make a direct cash donation to the charity. Or just donate your work and be satisfied with using your talents to help others.

When dealing with tough tax issues, it is always best to personally consult with a certified public accountant or tax attorney. You also can contact the IRS directly for help at 1-800-829-1040.

Doing Photography Work for Your Day-Job Employer

Conflicts may arise if you perform photography work for your day-job employer. These can be avoided if you make it clear that your photography company is performing the work, not you as an employee of the day-job. This is made easier if your photography business has an Employer Identification Number (EIN). Have your day-job employer pay your company using its EIN, not your social security number. Otherwise, the payment will be considered supplemental and be subject to extra withholding. While you may get the additional withholding back after you file your tax forms, a significant amount of the payment will be in the government's bank account, not yours until you get your tax refund. Having your day-job employer pay your photography business for work performed also avoids any conflict of interest issues and gives your photography additional clout.

Subcontracting Assistants

If you hire other photographers, make-up artists, reps, sales agents, or other persons on a temporary basis, you may need to establish a formal subcontractor relationship with them so that they will not be considered employees. The distinction is important because your state governs how employees can be fired and what employment taxes, such as FICA and worker compensation, will have to be paid.

Many factors are considered when determining whether a person assisting you is an employee or subcontractor. For example, the subcontractor sets her own hours, has a separate business entity, uses her own tools, and determines how to accomplish the task assigned. The employee is usually reimbursed for expenses, receives employee-type benefits, has no financial investment in the facilities used to perform the task, is paid a regular wage, and has an expectation for permanency of the relationship. Often, there is a written document to define the relationship, but that is not always conclusive. The IRS may find the relationship to be an employer-employee, depending on reasons like those listed.

Using a temporary agency to hire your assistants will better protect you by clearly defining your subcontractor relationship with the assistant. You hire the temporary agency, and the temp agency hires the worker. The temp agency then becomes the employer and is responsible for the employment taxes for the employee instead of you. It also helps to have a contract with a subcontractor so that you can define the responsibilities of the job and expectations of both parties.

If you need to hire employees instead of subcontractors, it is best to use an employment contract to define the relationship. Include all of the expectations and the parameters of the job in the contract. While many states provide for "employment at will" that allows you to fire an employee without cause, you still must adhere to legal restrictions when hiring or firing employees to avoid discrimination claims.

In sum, it's more expensive and complicated to hire an employee rather than a subcontractor. If you hire a subcontractor, be sure to maintain the relationship so that it never appears that the subcontractor is an employee. Otherwise, you will be subject to fines and penalties.

Agents

During your photographic career, you may find it beneficial to hire an agent. This allows you to concentrate on your photography while the agent concentrates on selling your work for a percentage of the income, usually from 10 to 15% for a book to around 25% for assignment work.

If you hire an agent, be extremely careful to define the expectations and parameters of the relationship. Your agent may be able to legally bind you to obligations and agreements.

An agent is considered to stand in your place. If the agent has "apparent authority," you may be legally required to fulfill obligations agreed to only by your agent. But if the agent goes beyond the contractually-defined relationship and does not have apparent authority, you will not be bound by the agent's action. While this will help you legally, be sure to hire an agent you trust so that he does not hurt your business relationships. You don't want to have to spend time getting out of deals even though the agent did not have the authority to make them for you.

Be sure to specifically define the market (location and type) where the agent can pitch your work and to include a list of your previous clients so that the agent will not receive a commission on sales to these parties. Also include a termination date for the relationship, whether it is for a year or with 30 days notice. You then must decide how commissions from clients secured by the agent will be handled after the termination. You may continue to pay the commissions for a limited time or may be able to pay a flat fee to buy out the contract. The time to think about these things is before they become a problem.

Invoices/Bills of Sale

When you sell your products or services to your clients, be sure to itemize exactly what you are selling on your invoices or bills of sale. First, it helps to justify your charges so that the client understands exactly what went into the work. Second, it provides evidence of your income and expenses for tax purposes. You also may qualify for a sales tax exemption because certain items are excluded from sales tax. If you don't itemize, then you can't calculate the amount of taxes owed.

For bookkeeping and marketing purposes, include your customer's name and address and the date on each invoice and give each invoice a unique number. That way you can track your client's activities and document the success of your marketing. Be sure also to include your terms and conditions on the invoice.

Bids and Estimates

Sometimes potential clients ask for a bid on a job; others will ask for an estimate. These two different items have important distinctions for photographers. A bid is a fixed price at which you will do the job. An estimate is your best guess at what a job will cost. The actual charge can be higher or lower than the estimate.

The bid should clearly identify the scope of work to be done—who, what, when and how. Don't just give a total for the job; itemize your bid, too. Itemization helps your client understand the steps necessary to complete the job and thus builds value. The more that is specified in the bid, the easier it will be to enforce your price. Also include a clause that allows you to substitute a photographer in your stead in case of death, illness, or injury to you.

When you submit a bid, list all exclusions in a prominent place on the bid. For example, you may not know all of the parameters of the job, such as how many days you are to work or how many models you are to shoot. If so, specifically note in your bid that it is based on the assumption that you will work for two days and shoot six models. You might include what the costs will be for additional days or models. Try to anticipate every variation on the job you are bidding on so that you will not do the work for less than you deserve. Your clients will be happier if they understand ahead of time what the full job will cost.

If the actual job is dramatically different than that bid upon, you may be able to get more pay. Check both your local laws and customs to see how bids are enforced.

Submit your bids in writing. Include a termination date for them, stating that the bid is valid through a specific date. If the bid is not accepted by then, the bid is void. Depending on the circumstances, bids should be valid for about ten days.

                                    Photographer's Legal Guide

Treat an estimate as carefully as you do a bid. Provide similar information and be realistic with your estimate. If your estimate is artificially high, you may not get the job. If it is inappropriately low, you run the risk of upsetting the client when you submit a much higher final bill. On that bill, include the original items so that the client can make a quick and easy comparison. Include a detailed explanation as to variances.

How you handle your bids and estimates can protect your interests, keep your clients happy, and increase your business.

Self Employment Issues

When you are self-employed you must pay employment, income, property, and sales tax yourself, usually on a quarterly basis. The paperwork can be daunting. If you don't maintain your records adequately or fail to pay on time, you can be subject to steep fines and penalties. Check with your local, state, and federal government to determine your reporting and payment requirements. You can get some help from the Small Business Administration with classes or educational materials, or you can hire a certified public accountant to take care of the work for you.

Maintain detailed records of your income and expenses and categorize them monthly. Keeping your files organized will allow your accountant to provide a more accurate record of your taxes due. If you are audited, then your good record keeping will serve you well.

Depending on your municipality, you may have to pay property tax on items that you use to conduct business. Keep a list of items used in your business, including the serial number, a description of the item, and the proof of purchase. You also can use this list to supply to your insurance company in case of loss.

Get Professional Legal Help

After reviewing various web forums and talking with folks, it is obvious that lots of photographers need help—professional legal help, that is. While the web is a wonderful tool, it has exacerbated the water-cooler rumor mill so that mis-information is rampant.

There is a reason why lawyers go to school for three full years and then have to take hours of continuing education each year. The law is a difficult, ever-changing and voluminous subject. A real estate attorney can't help you with a will and a divorce lawyer can't help you with a medical malpractice claim. It takes time and intense study to learn and to keep up with changes in the law. Each circumstance is unique; the law will affect each case in a different manner. You shouldn't take the advice of your neighbor's sister-in-law's cousin who talked to his uncle about how to prosecute a copyright infringement case. Even when the facts look similar, a lawyer is trained to find the nuances that may make or break your case.

The adage "penny wise, pound foolish" applies here. You can do a lot of your legal work yourself, but it will take lots of your time and you might get it wrong in the end. You've saved a few bucks upfront, but what will the costs be in the long run? Isn't your photography business important enough to get the best help? Should photographers risk their businesses with self-help or by following the advice of some guy who read an article on trademark law? Even the advice in this book is purely educational and does not purport to constitute legal advice. But hopefully it will encourage you to consult with a lawyer who can help you.

Hiring a Lawyer

Some hobbyist and most professional photographers will need the help of a lawyer at some point in their careers. You may want to locate one before you need one. If the need arises quickly, you will not be able to fully vet the attorney you hire.

The best way to find a lawyer is to get references. Talk with other photographers, business colleagues, friends, and neighbors to solicit their recommendations. When you get the names of several lawyers, review their credentials in Martindale Hubble (www.martindale.com), which is a national listing of most attorneys. Since not all attorneys are listed in Martindale, you may need to contact the attorney directly to ask for references and credentials. Make sure that you like and trust your attorney because you may have to give her a lot of money and spend a lot of time with her.

Just like doctors, many lawyers practice or specialize in certain areas, so it is best to find a lawyer who has experience with your particular issues. For photographers, this can range from copyright and trademark to employment and contract law. While you may hire one attorney to help you with certain needs, he may refer you to another lawyer for help in an area that is not his specialty. When you hire your lawyer, make sure that the agreement is in writing and that the agreement specifies what work is to be performed.

Paying for Legal Work

Lawyers can be paid in different ways. Most are paid on an hourly basis. In those cases, you may be required to pay a retainer, which is an advance on the amount that the lawyer expects that will be needed to complete the job. It assures the lawyer that you have the ability to pay in full for the work to be done. Retainers can be used for a specific case or issue or to cover a variety of needs whenever they arise. The lawyer is under an ethical duty to put those funds in an escrow account and may only withdraw the funds when the work is performed. Your lawyer must give you a periodical accounting of the status of the job, the amount of funds withdrawn and the amount remaining in the escrow account. When the work is completed, the lawyer will refund any remainder of the retainer after the account is cleared. If the retainer funds are exhausted, the lawyer may ask for another retainer or will bill you regularly for the additional work.

For work that generally takes a predictable amount of time, attorneys may charge a set or package rate. This is common for copyright and trademark registrations, preparation of simple wills, etc. Generally, the attorney will require payment in advance of any work performed for these tasks.

Some attorneys will take certain cases on a contingency basis; the lawyer will take a percentage of the recovery, if any. If there is no award or settlement, you usually owe the attorney only for the expenses, depending on the agreement that you have established with the lawyer. A normal contingency rate is a one-third of the recovery plus expenses if the case is settled before trial, and 40% plus expenses if the case goes to trial. Some lawyers require payment of the expenses as they are incurred. Typical expenses might include the consultation of experts, court fees, research, court reporters, and travel. Hiring an attorney on a contingency basis is a good alternative for a photographer who doesn't have enough money to pay a lawyer by the hour, but has a good case that will likely lead to a significant recovery. If the attorney takes your case on contingency, the attorney may ultimately earn more than if she had been paid on an hourly basis. But she is taking a risk by taking the case on a contingency basis as she may not be paid anything. A contingency case also provides extra incentive for the lawyer to get as high of an award as is possible. The disadvantage for you is that there may not be much money left after the expenses and attorneys are paid.

Working With Your Lawyer

After you hire an attorney, your work is not done. You can do a lot to help (or hurt) your case. Since you usually get one shot at winning a claim, here are 10 tips to make the most of your legal challenge:

1. Be candid. Your attorney can help you more if she knows the whole story, not just the good part or your side of things.

2. Be truthful. Lies can easily be exposed. Your case will be much stronger when you are honest.

3. Be responsive. If your lawyer asks you a question, answer it fully and directly. Follow directions from your lawyer.

4. Be accessible. Your attorney may need to talk with you without delay, so be available and return calls promptly.

5. Be discreet. Don't discuss your case with anyone other than your lawyer or her staff. While some information may be disclosed, it can be difficult to know when to talk and when to be quiet, so it is almost always best not to talk about your case to anyone but your lawyer.

6. Be reasonable. While you may have the best case in the world, sometimes it's better to cut your losses and get on with your life. The court system is designed to solve prob-

lems, whether through settlement or litigation. It is not the place to exact vengeance.

7. Be understanding. Your lawyer has other clients and almost surely has a personal life.

8. Be patient. The legal process takes much longer than the hour shown on TV. Some cases can take years, so don't expect immediate results.

9. Be kind. Treat your lawyer, her staff, and the opposing counsel with respect and consideration. They may be more reasonable when dealing with you and your claim.

10. Be realistic. The big verdict cases get a lot of publicity, but they are rare. Even with large awards, the money must first be used to pay court costs, attorney's fees, expert witness bills, deposition costs, etc.

Winning a case takes much more than just hiring a lawyer. It's a team effort. Follow these and other sound practices to help your legal team win.

Standing

Example: A client hires you to take pictures of a model. You own the copyrights to the photos, but the client subsequently claims that you cannot use them because you don't have a model release. Is the claim legally valid? Probably not.

For threats to be legally effective, the complainer must have "standing." Standing is the legal principle that states that persons may make claims for their own rights and not for someone else's rights. Unless the model in the scenario above is an employee of the client, the client has no standing and has no right to complain about your use of the photos. Only the model can sue you for possibly violating her rights.

While you don't want to anger clients, sometimes it's best to stand up for your rights. Make sure that the client has the standing needed to complain and has a valid complaint before you succumb to the client's threats.

Fear of Lawsuits

Photographers have certain rights but often are concerned about exercising those rights for fear of being sued. It's a legitimate concern because lawsuits can be costly and stressful, even when you win. The counter-concern is that if photographers don't exercise their rights, they may lose them.

Take, for example, the property release. The law does not require permission to take and use a photograph of property, so no release is required except when

    Photographer's Legal Guide

trademarks or copyrighted works are at issue. Most photographers understand that you may stand on publicly accessible land to take a photograph of a building without a release. But some photographers and users of photographs (such as stock agencies) will want a property release to use the photograph of that building to allay concerns of being sued. Some may require one only if the photograph is used commercially. Will it hurt to get one? Not in the short run, but there may be a long term negative effect.

If the building's owner signs the property release, then you have little concern that he will sue you for the use of the photo (but it is still a possibility). But what if he refuses to sign? Then you will have to find another building to photograph and ask for permission again. What if he demands payment? You then must pay for something that you are entitled to have for free.

If the building owner signs the release, he will expect the next photographer to ask for a property release, too. If permission is not requested, will the owner sue the second photographer for doing something within his rights? Will all photographers then have to get permission or pay for something when it is not legally required?

What other photographers' rights will erode from fear of exercising them? The first step towards protecting your rights is to know them. The second is to stand up for them.

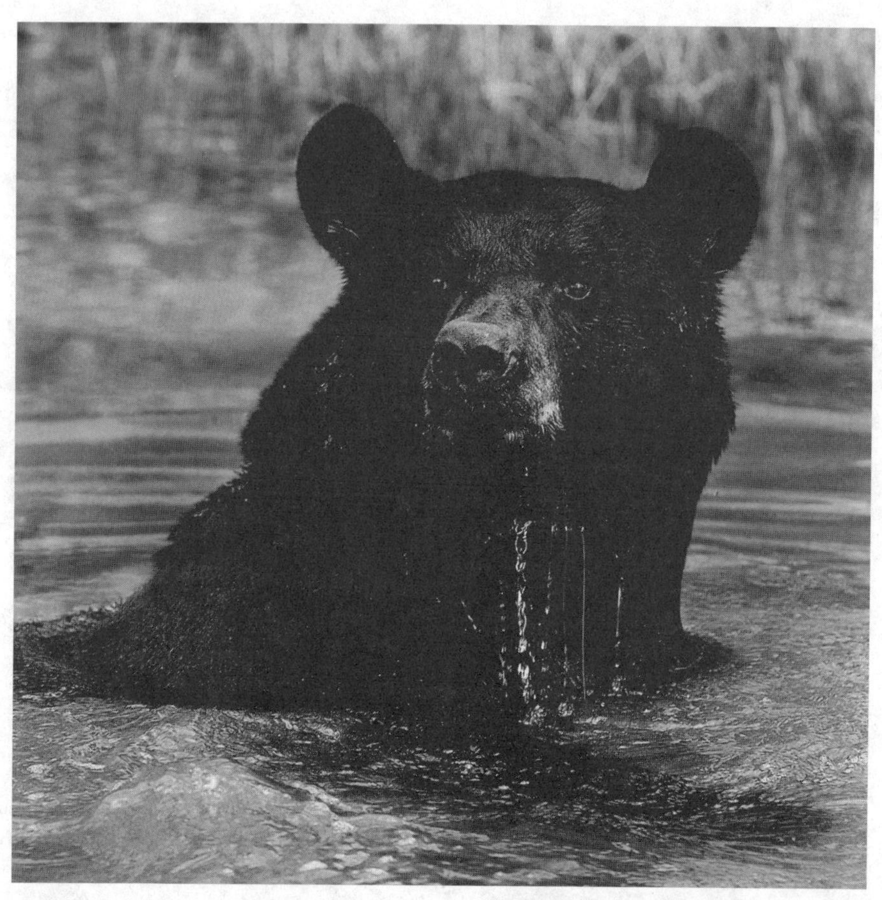

Copyright 2005 Carolyn E. Wright

Photographer's Legal Guide

Getting Paid For Your Photography

Getting Paid

Photography equipment is expensive and your time is valuable. While some may want to provide their photography services for free, it is important for photographers who are making it a business to get fair compensation for their work. Because so many people own cameras, photographers sometimes have an uphill battle to get the recognition and payment they deserve.

The key is to prevent problems before they occur. Never give your product to a client until you are paid in full. Follow this policy even for friends, because it can be harder to ask for overdue payments from them. You are not allowed to walk out of a department store with a shirt, and it should not be different with your business. Get used to asking for (and demanding if need be) and collecting your payments up front. You want to avoid making the client angry by pursuing payment or cheating yourself out of being paid what is due. If you run your business like a business, both your friends and clients will treat it that way.

You can greatly increase your chances of getting paid if you have a good contract that covers all of the bases. Your agreement should include all of the specifics regarding payment—who pays, when he pays, how he pays and how much he pays. When this is spelled out in the beginning, there can be no surprises, you will receive fewer complaints, and you increase your likelihood of being paid appropriately. If your client balks at signing an agreement that clearly spells out each of your obligations, walk away from the job before you get stiffed.

When to Get Paid

It's best to arrange in the contract to be paid in advance, at least for part of the job. Being paid a portion of the total amount due is standard in the industry for assignment work. Always insist on full payment before giving images to the client. If the client is given the product without completing his payment, he has no incentive to pay you. You may choose to give discounts for advance or for early payments. In those rare cases when you arrange to be paid on credit, be strict about those terms and enforce the penalties for late payment.

Depending on the local customs for non-commercial work, it's good practice to include a liquidated damages clause (see more in the Contracts chapter) so that you are compensated for your reserved time if the client reschedules. Get your clients to acknowledge the requirement by specifically including it in your agreement. Explain its purpose to your clients by telling them that you have blocked time for them when you could have booked other work. This is especially true during peak wedding season. For portrait sessions, you may want to charge a re-booking fee when clients cancel a scheduled shoot instead of asking for liquidated damages. That encourages the clients to go forward with the session at a later date instead of canceling it entirely.

Payment schedules also vary by industry and type of job as follows:

Weddings

For weddings, it is customary for the client to prepay in full for your services. You may want to require a retainer to hold the wedding date, and then collect the rest of the full payment before the wedding. This is especially important for weddings because the bride and groom frequently become financially overextended for the big event. After the ceremony, you may have to compete with the florist or caterer for your money. You won't have to wait in line if you get paid in advance.

Portraits

For portrait sessions, you usually get half of the sitting fee before the shoot and the remainder upon delivery of the photos. Reprints are paid for upon delivery.

Magazines

Prepayment rarely works here. Magazines often "pay on publication," so you don't get paid until the magazine hits the newsstand. Some magazines "pay upon acceptance" of the image to be published. In most cases when you are working with established entities, you have to adapt to their policies.

Government/Large Business

Government entities or large businesses are often slow to pay. It can take quite a while to get through the red tape, so be prepared either to wait to get paid or simply do not accept them as clients.

Credit Checks on Clients

When it looks as if you may be doing a lot of work for a new client, you may want to determine whether the client has the resources to pay you. This can be as simple as checking with other photographers who have done work for the client or as complex as using resources to run extensive credit checks on the client.

Generally, the longer a company has been in business, the higher the likelihood that it will be able to pay you. You also can ask clients for credit, bank or trade references. Then contact the references to verify everything you have been told is accurate. Make sure the potential clients are who they say they are. Ask the references whether the client pays on time and whether the client owes them money.

If the client is a large business, you can review Dunn & Bradstreet reports on the company. You also can get credit reports online from Experian, TransUnion or

TRW. If your client is a sole proprietor, you can do background checks on the owner using the web.

Unless you want to give your photography services away for free, you should make sure that the client can pay you. If you can't verify the client's credit worthiness, then do the work only when the client will pay in advance.

Partial Payments

If you get into a dispute with a client about your product or the amount due, then try to get at least a partial payment. Tell the client that you'll work the rest out later. First, that gets you at least something for the work done. Second, you then may be able to collect the whole amount because a court may determine that the client waived the right to dispute the issue. Even if the client marks "payment in full" on the check or in the documentation that comes with the payment, the client's unilateral attempt to conclude the issue will be unsuccessful. Go ahead and cash the check and then go after your client to collect the rest that you are owed.

Dunning Letters for Late Payments

If your client doesn't pay your invoice, you will have to decide how aggressively you want to pursue payment. A "dunning" letter is a great tool that can help you to collect payments, especially when client relationships are sensitive. A dunning letter is a friendly but firm reminder that the client owes you money. Include in the letter the consequences to the client if payment isn't delivered. These might include interest, a flat fee surcharge, the forfeit of discounts, the possibility of a lawsuit, turnover of the payment due to a collection agency, and/or the loss of the business relationship. Send a second letter, if necessary. These consequences of non-payment should be included in each contract so that your client will know that you mean business.

Dealing with Non-Payment

Even if you follow the above advice, you may not get paid. How you proceed depends on several factors. Do you want to continue the relationship? If so, you should try to collect with less aggression. If it was a one-time deal and/or you don't care about damaging the relationship, then you can be more assertive with the collection process.

When it comes to collecting on past due accounts, the squeaky wheel gets the grease. While you may be afraid to dispute the issue with your client for fear that you'll lose their business, you should be more concerned about losing your own business if your clients don't pay. Attain the reputation as a photographer who won't work for free.

Penalties that you impose for late payments cannot be "usury" or excessive. They should be in line with the actual costs of the non-payment, such as current interest rates, collection and attorney fees, etc.

Be careful when collecting debts yourself. The U.S. Fair Debt Collection Practices Act (15 U.S.C. 1601 et seq.) places some limits on what you can do to collect. You cannot harass your client with late-night phone calls or ask the client's friends or relatives to pay the debt.

Collection Agencies

If you don't care about continuing the relationship with the non-paying client, you may want to turn the debt over to a collection agency. While it will cost you money, a collection agency is generally much more effective than you will be at collecting debts. It has the resources and systems designed to specifically to find the client's assets and seize them. A collection agency is especially helpful when the debtor is out of state. A collection agency's standard cut is 15 to 50% of the debt, but in general they will be able to collect the debt so that you will recover some of the money due you. To find a reputable and ethical collection agency, contact the American Collectors Association at http://www.acainternational.org/ or the Commercial Law League of America at http://www.clla.org/. Lawyers also can be hired to collect debts. Remember that every minute you spend trying to collect on a bad debt means that you're not making money from another client.

Going to Court

If your claim is small and the client is local, consider filing a claim in "magistrate" or small claims court to collect the debt. You usually don't need to hire an attorney to pursue your claim and the court personnel will often help you fill out the forms. In fact, many states don't allow lawyers in their small claims courtrooms. Contact your small claims court to ascertain its filing requirements.

If attorneys are allowed to represent clients in small claims court and your client has legal representation, you should get a lawyer, too. You also may want to get your own lawyer if your case is complicated or if you are uncomfortable representing yourself.

The amount that you can collect in small claims court varies from state to state. Some have minimums starting at $1,000 and all have maximums ranging up to $10,000. Even if you're owed more than the maximum, you can forego the excess and seek the maximum allowed by the court.

If your deadbeat client resides in a different county than you, you may have to use that county's small claims court. Where you can file your claim depends on a variety of factors, such as where the contract was made and where the work was done. If you are in doubt as to where to file, seek guidance from an attorney or the court. You can, however, always can sue defendants where they (or where the company) is located.

                    Photographer's Legal Guide

If your claim is large, hire a lawyer to take your debt-dodging client to court. Your attorney usually will take a 30% to 40% cut of the collections after expenses are deducted. Doing so will help establish your reputation as a photographer who demands prompt payment. Otherwise, you'll be known as a photographer who will work for free.

Even after you get a judgment in small claims or state court, it does not guarantee that you will collect on the debt. Your attorney can help you with post-judgment collection by garnishing wages, seizing property, or attaching liens to bank accounts.

Arbitration/Mediation

Sometimes when you are hired for a photography job, you will be required to sign a contract that includes an arbitration or mediation clause. The clause provides that the method for settling all contractually-related disputes will be by arbitration or mediation. Each of these methods has pros and cons. Analyze them carefully with the help of an attorney before signing on the dotted line.

ARBITRATION

Arbitration can be binding or non-binding. If it is binding, you are stuck with the decision of the arbiter. If it is not binding, you still have the right to pursue your claim in court if you don't like the arbiter's decision. Do not agree to an arbitration clause that allows the client to choose the arbitrator, especially for binding arbitration. See additional information about arbitration in the Contracts chapter. Arbitration generally favors the client/defendant, so be especially careful before agreeing to it.

MEDIATION

Mediation is becoming a common way of settling disputes. It involves an unbiased, court-appointed or privately-hired mediator who attempts to get the parties to resolve their differences by coming to a mutual agreement. Since mediation is not binding, you commit only your time and usually the shared cost of the mediator. It can be a civilized way to reach a settlement. If the mediation is not successful, you retain your ability to go to court.

Credit Cards

To provide payment options for your clients, to expand your business beyond your location, and to give the appearance of a professional business, you may need to accept credit cards in some form. But there are legal and business ramifications that come with accepting credit cards for payments. Consider these carefully before committing to the setup and processing fees.

When you accept credit cards, you pay a small fee for the use of the credit card, usually 3 to 5% or a bit less, depending on your credit worthiness. You also are subject to federal and state laws that govern the use and acceptance of credit cards. Another concern with accepting credit cards is that customers can challenge a charge within 30 days. Not only do these "charge-backs" come with a fee, you may lose the entire payment the client made despite having performed the work.

To set up a credit card account, go to your bank or find a bank that will set up a "merchant account" for your business. Be wary of credit card/merchant account offers from websites and solicitations by mail and phone. Some banks no longer offer credit card processing, or they may be unwilling to provide the service to a small business. In those cases, ask your bank to refer you to an independent sales organization that will help you find a credit card processor. The bank also may be able to help you get the required processing equipment and the training needed to accept credit cards.

Don't set up merchant status to share with a friend. It is the same as co-signing on a loan, and you can be personally responsible for all of the liabilities incurred by your friend related to the merchant activities.

Be sure to follow all of the transaction guidelines carefully whether you process the cards in person or electronically. When you make a physical imprint of [or when you swipe] the card to process the payment, you will pay a smaller transaction fee because that method is less of a security risk. If you accept credit cards online, get your customer's name as it appears on card, the complete billing address, and the 3 or 4 digit verification numbers. If you have two of these three items, then you can usually defeat a dispute claiming that the charge was fraudulent.

PayPal

Merchant status—the ability to accept credit cards—is governed by your credit worthiness. If you have credit problems, using PayPal may be your only resort. Regardless, it is becoming a common method of payment.

PayPal works well for those selling prints online. PayPal also lets you send an invoice or money to anyone with an email address. It is free for those purchasing goods and services and works with the purchaser's existing credit card or checking accounts.

As with any business, there have been complaints about PayPal's operations. These include unfairly and improperly restricting accounts or having a less than effective back-up system. But there are few alternatives for person-to-person online payments. PayPal is a "money transmitter," not a bank. It may be subject to state regulations as a transmitter, but is not governed by federal banking protections and your funds are not FDIC insured.

Almost without exception, you are subject to the agreement that you enter into with PayPal. Here are some tips to follow when using PayPal's services:

- PayPal offers a Seller Protection Policy that provides security for your transactions; the terms must be strictly followed. You should only accept PayPal payments from customers with an address in the United States that is "confirmed" by PayPal. Check PayPal's website for additional requirements.

- PayPal provides teams to review chargebacks and fraudulent activities that are not protected by the Seller Protection Policy. Follow PayPal's guidelines carefully for the best protection.

- Review PayPal's policy on fraud protection.

- Don't leave large sums of money in your Paypal account. PayPal will transfer the funds to your affiliated bank account for free, but it may take a few days. PayPal earns interest off of those funds but doesn't pass the interest onto you.

- Limit the amount of funds that you have in the affiliated bank account. PayPal may be able to access that money in cases that are disputed.

- Use PayPal for small purchases. Consider an escrow service for larger transactions or use certified checks, money orders or wire transfers.

Money Orders

Some money orders can be as worthless as a bad check. They can be cancelled or they may be fraudulent. Treat them like checks; make sure they clear the bank before you ship your product.

Domestic money orders from the U.S. Postal Service are safe and economical. The maximum amount of a postal money order is $1,000, but you can purchase up to ten of those per day. They are valid for an unlimited time, can be cashed at any post office or bank, and will be replaced if damaged, lost or stolen.

You can safely accept international money orders for payment as long as they are in U.S. dollars. They are especially reliable if they are "International Postal Money Orders" issued by countries that have entered into agreements with the U.S. Postal Service in accordance with the policies and requirements located at http://pe.usps.gov/text/Imm/immc3_007.html. The maximum amount that will be protected per money order differs in each country. Since there is no limit on the number of money orders you can use, you may combine money orders when the amount due is over the protected limit. Otherwise, make sure that the funds are deposited into your account without restrictions before delivering your work to the client.

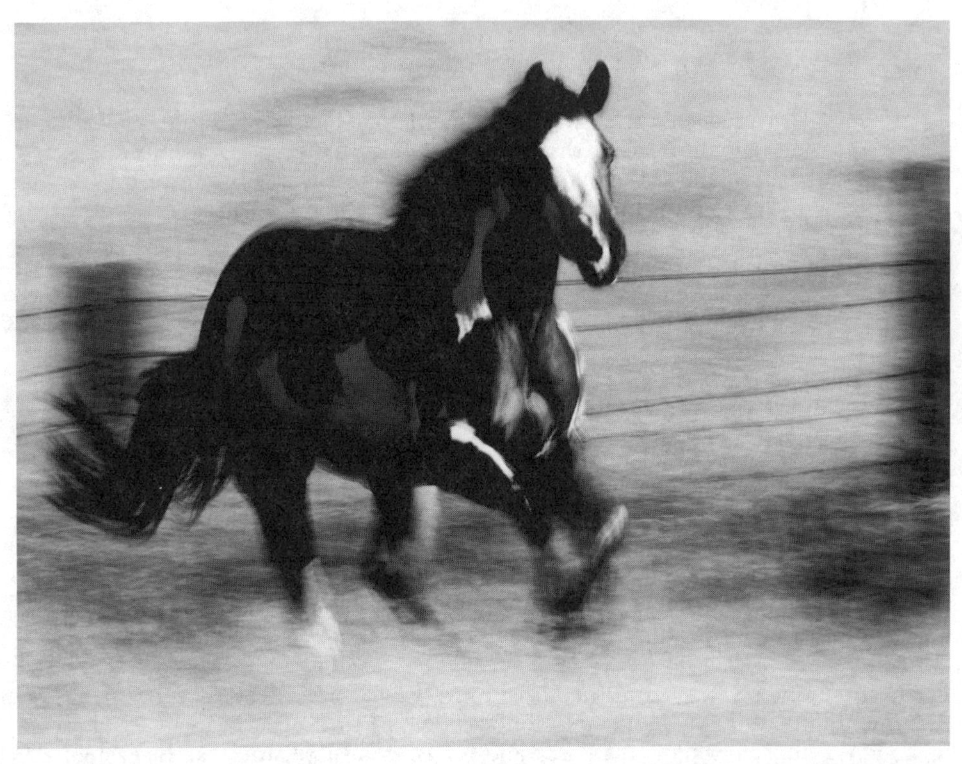

Copyright 2005 Carolyn E. Wright

                              Photographer's Legal Guide

Insurance For Photographers

Liability Insurance

There are risks inherent in business of any kind and photographers need to protect themselves just as any other business person would. If you set up a studio in your home and a client is injured on your property, you can be sued. If a judgment is entered against you, your home can be used ("attached") to pay the damages. Likewise, if you establish your photography business as one that exposes your personal assets to liabilities (such as a sole proprietorship or a partnership), your home and any other personal property can be attached regardless of where the injury occurs.

You should not rely on your homeowners insurance for your photography business. Home insurance policies often have specific exclusions for claims that are made in conjunction with commercial activity conducted there. Be sure to purchase insurance that specifically covers your business activities whether they are conducted in your home or elsewhere.

Make sure that the liability policy covers all areas of your photography business. This is especially important if you are a location photographer. If you are photographing a wedding or leading a photography workshop, you need liability insurance in case someone is injured from a slip and fall or property is damaged. Errors and omissions insurance, including media liability coverage, encompasses mistakes that you make while doing your work. It basically is malpractice insurance for photographers. If you accidentally erase the images from an entire wedding from your computer or if you forget to show up for an event, then an errors and omissions policy will cover some or all of the legal fees for your defense against a lawsuit and will usually pay all or part of the judgment or settlement. Wedding and portrait photographers in particular are vulnerable to these types of claims.

If you opt for a standard business or commercial policy, make sure that it is written by reputable, well-known company. Viable alternatives may be available from various photography associations such as the American Society of Media Photographers ("ASMP"), Editorial Photographers ("EP"), or Professional Photographers of America ("PPA"). These groups often have relationships with insurance companies that offer the types of coverages to meet the needs of photographers at reduced rates.

Insurance Tips

When selecting a company to provide your insurance policy, be careful. You usually will not learn that an agent is corrupt or that an insurance policy is faulty or invalid until you need coverage, when it is too late. Information on insurance companies is often available from the Better Business Bureau or from the state's insurance commissioner's office, but a recommendation from another photographer may be best. If you get your insurance from an unlicensed company, then your policy isn't worth the paper it's written on.

Be sure to read the proposed policy carefully yourself before your buy it; do not rely on what the agent tells you that the policy covers. Make sure there are no exclusions that might prove critical to your business. Be sure also to read any notices or revisions that are sent to you after you have bought your policy to make sure that the changes won't affect the coverage you need.

When setting your insurance policy limits, choose the highest deductible and the most protection that you can afford. Insurance is designed for those losses that will jeopardize the continued existence of your business and is best used only when absolutely necessary. Don't use it as a savings account to cover minor incidents.

Don't make claims for petty losses; otherwise, your insurance company may drop you or increase your payments so much that you can't afford to continue to pay the premiums. You may lose a lot more than you gain if you make claims for small losses.

You may be able to purchase insurance that covers the loss of data—your images, slides, negatives, etc.,—but if you can find it, it will be expensive. Consider it only if you have a valuable collection. Backing up your data or storing slide dupes off site is a much cheaper alternative.

Disability Insurance

Disability insurance is especially important for those photographers who are self-employed. If you get sick or injured, you will need insurance to cover your loss of income. This can be difficult for new photographers to get as it is usually tied to past income. Explore your options by checking with various photography organizations or the Small Business Association in your area.

Insurance Coverage for Your Property and Equipment

Photographers' equipment is often stolen or damaged. To protect yourself against such losses, you will need to have your equipment insured either as part of, or separate from, your liability policy. These types of policies should provide for the replacement of your costly equipment in the event of a loss.

Because the value of photography equipment, especially the value of digital cameras and computers, decreases rapidly, you may want to cover only the cost of replacing your equipment. Standard insurance policies will reimburse you for the current value of the equipment at the time of the loss, although it will cost you much more to buy the newest version of the photography equipment. Replacement coverage instead will pay for the new, more expensive, substitute item.

                    Photographer's Legal Guide

An all-risk, complete replacement policy is often called "inland marine" coverage. It covers losses of any kind, such as theft or damage, even when you cause the damage (accidentally). While it is more expensive than other types of insurance coverage, it is great to have this coverage for your costly equipment such as lenses and camera bodies. To save money, insure only your most expensive equipment with an inland marine policy and the rest with a standard contents insurance policy.

If you have employees, be sure that your policy covers the theft of your equipment by an employee. You also should cover more than just your cameras. Fire or flood could damage everything that you use to do your business. Determine what it would cost you to replace it all. That's what you will need to cover. Review your insurance coverage yearly to make sure that it's up to date. Be sure to update your list of covered equipment by deleting items that have either been sold or are no longer in use, and by adding newly purchased items.

If you operate your photography business in a commercial building, then you will need insurance that specifically covers you and possibly the landlord, as well (depending on the terms of your lease). Review the lease requirements carefully.

Self Insurance

To prevent losses, use common sense to protect yourself and your equipment. This is the best way to protect yourself against loss. Handle your equipment carefully. Don't lend it to others who might abuse or mistreat it. Don't leave it unattended in a car or hotel room. Be discreet when showing it in public, even on a job where the public is present. Maintain and service your equipment so that it keeps its value. Use reliable equipment. And deal with reputable photo processors.

Photography can be a physical business, so be sure to keep yourself healthy. Keep your work area safe and free of obstacles. Check your employee references carefully so that you have reliable and trustworthy support personnel.

Back up your computer files and keep copies off site. Don't connect the computer or drives on which you store your images to the internet or else use reliable virus software and set up a firewall to keep them safe.

As a photographer, you must do all that you can to protect yourself and your work.

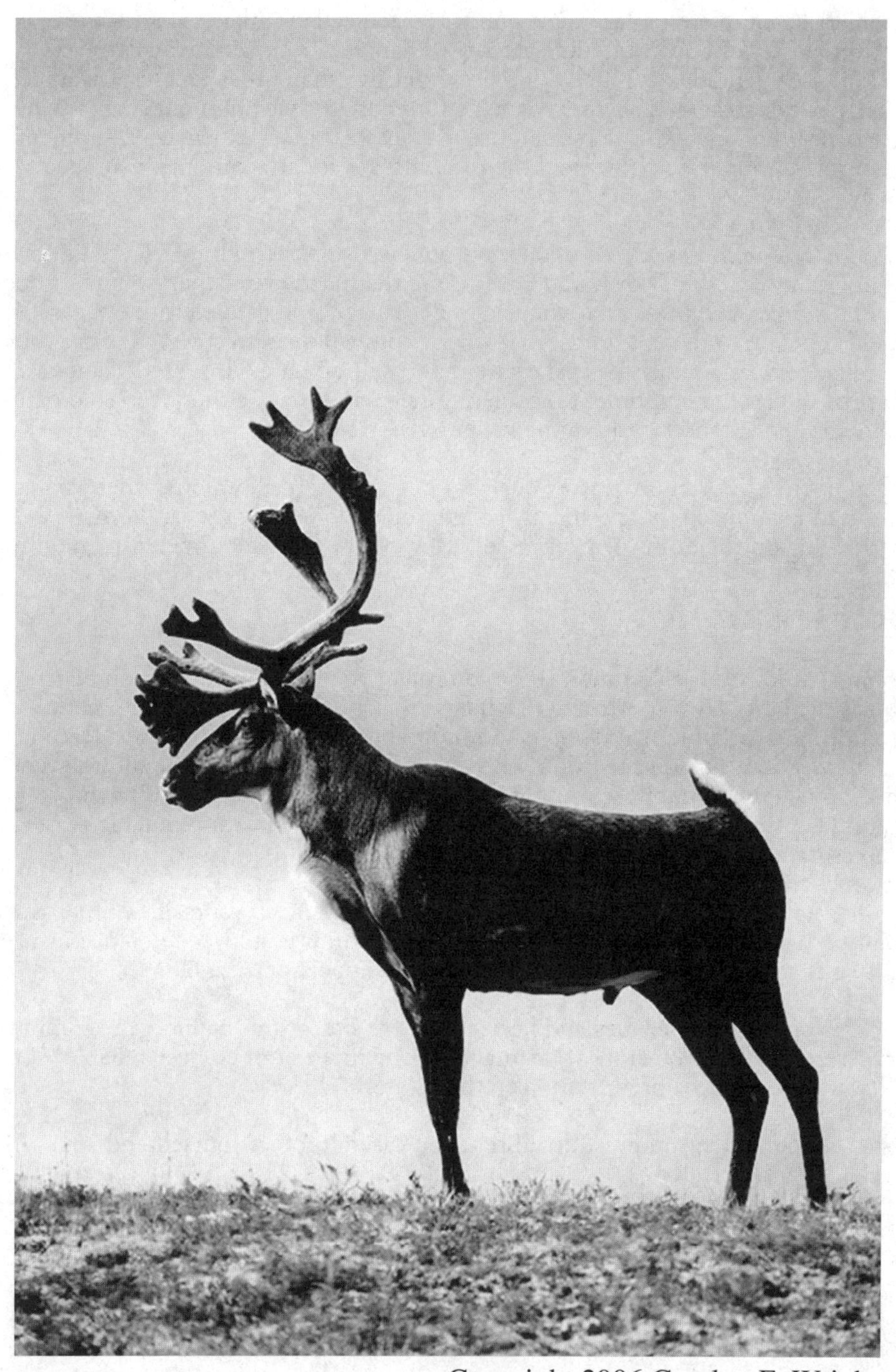

Copyright 2006 Carolyn E. Wright

COPYRIGHTS FOR PHOTOGRAPHERS

Copyright – What Is It?

Intellectual Property (IP) is property for which the owner has specific legal rights, just like your car, house and camera equipment. But IP is intangible; you cannot touch it. IP includes copyrights, trademarks, patents, and trade secrets. While similar, these types of IP have distinct differences. Patents are novel and non-obvious inventions that "do" something useful. Trademarks identify sources of products. Trade secrets are confidential business items that are not easily obtained by someone outside your business; they usually give your business an advantage in the market. Copyright is a legal form of protection granted by the U.S. Constitution for original works that include literary, dramatic, musical, artistic and photographic works. Copyright gives the author or creator the exclusive "right" to "copy" the original work. Generally, photographers are most concerned with copyrights and, to a lesser extent, with trademarks. Copyrights do not extend to ideas, methods, procedures, concepts, principles, short names, titles, slogans, and works that have not been transformed into a tangible or form, such as a print or electronic file.

It is important for photographers to understand what is protected by copyright. For example, you're in beautiful Yosemite National Park. On your way to the Mariposa Groves you pull into a parking lot next to a tunnel. You look to your right and see the splendor of Yosemite Valley including Bridal Veil Falls, Half Dome, and El Capitan. Of course, you want to photograph the scene.

But wait. Look down closely and you'll see the thousands of tripod leg indentations. It's been done before, and done well by none other than Ansel Adams. So when you make an image similar to "Tunnel View," is that copyright infringement?

Copyright law protects original expressions, not ideas. So when Mr. Adams had the idea to photograph Tunnel View, he owned the copyright to the expression of that idea only. That is, his copyright covers the photograph, not the subject matter. So then it's perfectly OK to photograph Tunnel View, right? Well, there's more.

It's clear to most everyone that you can't photocopy Mr. Adams' photograph. But did you know that his copyright protects more than just the exact image? Copyright law also protects his expression of the subject including the elements of his composition, the lighting, the shading, the camera angle, the background, and the perspective.

The parking lot at Tunnel View is small and allows few options to photographers. If you create an image of the same scene and include some of the same elements of Mr. Adams' composition, does that constitute infringement? It would only if you produced something "substantially similar" to his work. And it would if the average person on the street thought that your image was basically the same as Mr. Adams copyrighted image.

You place a copy of Adam's "Tunnel View" photograph next to your camera and do everything that you can to create precisely the same image. You state that you are attempting to make an exact copy of his photograph. Are you guilty of copyright infringement yet? It depends; again, would an ordinary person find that you were successful in copying his image to a meaningful degree? Probably not. The trees in the area are different, the weather and the quality of the light change from moment to moment, and Mr. Adams had skills that most do not have.

This test of whether you have infringed Mr. Adams' copyright is made easier by copyright law. Photographs of objects as they occur in nature are not protected by copyright law because they are ever-changing. So feel free to photograph all of the natural icons; you are not in danger of infringing anyone's copyrights. But when it comes to photographing all other objects, check these tests to ensure that you're respecting the copyrights of others.

Rights of the Copyright Owner

A copyright is created at the moment a work is made into a fixed form. For photographers, it is created at the click of the shutter. Your photograph is protected by copyright regardless of whether it is recorded on film or digitally. Images on the web are protected by copyrights, just as your prints are. Copyright law protects both unpublished photos and published photos, regardless of whether they have been registered with the U.S. Copyright Office.

Copyrights give the owner the exclusive right to do, or to authorize others to do, specific things with the photographs. Copyright law effectively gives you, the copyright owner, a legal monopoly on the use of that image. It also gives the copyright owner the right to prevent someone else from destroying their work.

When you own a copyright, you have the sole right to:

·   reproduce the copyrighted work;

·   display the copyrighted work publicly;

·   prepare derivative works based on the copyrighted work; and

·   distribute copies of the copyrighted work to the public by
       sale, rental or lending, and/or to display the image.

These "exclusive rights" may be assigned, sold, transferred or given away. When you assign, sell, transfer or give away any part of these rights, you may do so verbally. When you transfer the copyright in total to someone else, you must do so in writing.

                    Photographer's Legal Guide

Licensing your work verbally can, however, cause problems. Imagine the surprise of art collector, Duke Prentup, when he found that the $100 lithograph he purchased from University of Colorado Professor Ward Churchill was a mirror image of a pen and ink drawing by well-known artist, Thomas E. Mails, entitled "The Mystic Warriors of the Plains." While Mr. Prentup likes Churchill's lithograph, he is now disappointed with his purchase.

The two pieces are nearly identical; it is clear that the lithograph was copied. The question is: Did Mails, the copyright owner, give Churchill permission to prepare a derivative work? We may never know; Mails is deceased. His son believes that his father would never have given such permission. Because such permission can be given verbally, there may not be a record and no written record has been found. Unfortunately, the son's opinion would not carry much weight in court.

What can we learn from this story? Always put it in writing when you allow some to use your work. Make it a standard practice so that even after you're gone, your heirs will be able to testify that your licenses were always written. That type of testimony would carry weight in the courtroom. Always having a written license that documents what rights you are granting to someone else is the best way to protect your copyrighted work.

The Limits of Copyright Law

Copyright law is not absolute; it provides certain exceptions. For example, you cannot copyright an idea, but only the expression of that idea. If you decide to photograph a red rose against a black velvet background, your rendition of that scene is copyrighted. No one can publish, sell, display, manipulate or distribute that picture without your permission. However, someone else can take your idea and go to the local flower shop, buy a red rose, and photograph it against a black background. There is—of course—nothing you can do to stop them as long as the rendition of the scene is not substantially similar to yours. There are other exceptions to copyright protection, as well. One is the right of fair use.

Fair Use

The limits of copyright law are evident if you look at an image of a city street. Look closely and you'll see copyrighted material everywhere in your photo: on the billboards, on the covers of magazines in the newsstand, and the statue in front of the building. You would never be able to track down all of the copyright owners to get their permission to create a derivative work.

Though copyright law can be restrictive when it comes to photography, it is not irrational. Copyright law includes the doctrine of "fair use;" this allows the unauthorized use of copyrights in certain circumstances. The courts recognize that free expression and avoiding law suits over minor issues are more important than protecting intellectual property rights.

The doctrine of fair use means that copying will not infringe a copyright when it is "for purposes such as criticism, comment, news reporting, teaching, scholarship or research." Four factors are considered to determine whether the inclusion of copyrighted works in a photograph qualifies under the doctrine of fair use:

· The purpose and character of the use, including whether such use is of a commercial nature or is for nonprofit or for educational purposes;

· The nature of the copyrighted work;

· The amount and substantiality of the copyrighted material that is used; and

· The effect of the use upon the potential market for or value of the copyrighted work.

If the copyrighted material that appears in your photo satisfies an examination of the fair use tests, you do not have to be concerned with getting permission to use it. It is always a judgment call. Would a court agree with your position? It might be costly to find out. An alternative would be to get the advice of a copyright lawyer. The lawyer can give you an opinion based on research and experience.

Under the doctrine of fair use, courts have determined that a search engine website may include a thumbnail of your photograph. News services can use your photos when reporting on a story. Others may use your image for parody. A teacher may be able to use some of your work for educational purposes. Defining the boundaries of fair use is sometimes difficult and at times can be subject to litigation. But the safest and surest way to use copyrighted work in a photograph is to get permission in writing from the copyright owner.

Who Owns the Copyright

Joint Copyrights

In general, when the shutter is released, the photographer who pressed the button owns the copyright. Photographers, however, often work with others when making their photographs such as art directors, stylists, assistants, or even Photoshop editors. Does that person share the copyright with the photographer? It depends.

If the work done by the other person would not qualify on its own to be copyrightable, then the copyright is not jointly held without following the requirements noted below. Even though two people intended to create a unified work, the copyright will not automatically be shared. For example, when the art director suggests that a model pose on the hood of a red car, that "idea" is not copyrightable. When the photographer shoots the model posed on the hood of the red car, the photographer solely owns the copyright to the image unless the

   Photographer's Legal Guide

photographer and the art director agreed in writing that the copyright would be jointly held.

If a photograph's copyright is to be jointly held with someone other than the photographer, both the photographer and the contributors must have intended at the time the photograph was created that they be joint authors. Specifically, the Copyright Act of 1976 states that a joint copyright is "a work prepared by two or more authors with the intention that their contributions be merged into inseparable or inter-dependent parts of a unitary whole." This is important because when you share the copyright of a photograph with others, you have to agree on how it is to be licensed. Once it is licensed, the profits must be shared.

Regardless of the law, however, a person who contributed to the creation of your image may make a claim for joint ownership of the copyright. While you should be able to thwart those efforts, it could cost you time and money and create ill will, as well. Be sure that any agreements you sign give you sole ownership of the copyright. And when you hire assistants or Photoshop editors, have a signed agreement in place stating that you retain sole ownership of the copyrights regardless of the work performed by the assistant or the editor.

Work-for-Hire

A photographer owns the copyright for images that they create, unless the creation of those images falls into the "work-for-hire" category. A work-for-hire relationship is created in two situations: (1) the photographer is an employee hired to photograph for the employer—an example would be a photojournalist who is an employee of a newspaper; or (2) the photographer is hired to provide photographs for collective works or compilations and signs a written agreement that specifically states that the work is to be considered a work made for hire. Therefore, freelance photographers are subjected to work-for-hire status only when they agree to it contractually. Work-for-hire provisions are usually negotiable and monetary considerations should be included when photographers are asked to give up their copyrights.

Licensing Your Copyright

If you give a slide to a publisher, email a digital file to a client, or sell a print at an art show, you have not transferred your copyright unless stated so specifically in a written agreement that you have signed. Instead, you have given the recipient "non-exclusive rights;" you still own the copyright to the image. But when you transfer the copyright in writing to another party, you relinquish all rights to the image. It is as if you never took the photograph.

Non-exclusive rights may be transferred without a written agreement. However, just as it helps to have any agreement in writing so that all parties understand what is being agreed to, it is beneficial to also grant non-exclusive rights in writing. When you grant specific, limited rights to an image while maintaining ownership of the copyright, you have licensed the image. For example, you can give a magazine the limited right to print one of your photos. You send the image to the publisher and state that you are granting the magazine specific limited rights to use the image. You might give the magazine the one-time right to print 100,000 copies of the magazine or the right to use the image for a defined period of time. For a portrait, wedding or event photography business, you may give copies of the images to your clients so that they can have prints made. If you do that, be sure to limit their rights to personal use only so that they can not license the images to the Enquirer.

Licensing your images is like eating your cake and having it too. You can license the same image over and over again but keep the copyright. Unless you state specifically in writing and sign the document that transfers the copyright of an image to someone else, you own the copyright.

Copyright Licensing Issues

When you own the copyright of a photograph, you have complete and exclusive control of how it is reproduced, displayed and distributed. These rights may be assigned, sold, transferred or given away. If you decide to authorize others to use or to license your copyright, you should consider the following:

- Who are you giving the rights to?

- What specific rights are you granting?

- Are you authorizing print rights, electronic rights, or both? If you grant electronic rights, are they for CD, web, or other uses?

- For how long are you granting the rights?

- Will the rights be exclusive?

- How will the rights be used? In what markets or industries?

- What territory is covered by the rights? North America? English-speaking countries? Worldwide?

- Are there any work-for-hire implications?

- How will you be paid? By a flat fee? By royalties? If paid by royalties, how will the royalties be calculated?

- When will you be paid?

- Will you allow certain alterations of the work to be made?

- Will you require that a copyright notice or a photo credit be included?

- Who will be responsible for loss, damage, or theft of the work?

- Will you require samples or tear sheets?

- Specifically retain all other rights to your copyrights: "All rights not specifically granted herein remain with the photographer." You never know what future usage technology might bring.

- Make the license subject to being paid in full: "Until we have agreed to the terms included here and you have paid the agreed-upon fee, you have no right to use the work. Any unauthorized use shall constitute infringement."

While licensing rights can be done verbally, it is—of course—best to put them in writing. You will minimize confusion and have something concrete to rely upon if a dispute arises. To be sure that every important aspect of licensing is addressed, ask an attorney who is familiar with these issues to review the license.

Licensing Terminology

If the language used to license copyrights is not specific enough, the photographer and the licensee might not agree as to what rights have been granted. Thanks to the PLUS Coalition, much of this confusion may be avoided in the future.

PLUS (Picture Licensing Universal System) is an international non-profit trade association whose goal is "to simplify and facilitate the licensing of images." The Coalition consists of photographers, illustrators, stock picture agencies, artist representatives, advertising agencies, advertisers, graphic design firms, publishers, attorneys, and associated industries. Through PLUS, licensors and licensees are working together "to provide a single, comprehensive resource for use by every professional engaged in licensing images so that we all may speak a common language, avoid misunderstandings, and achieve a precise mutual understanding of the scope of any image license."

The PLUS Coalition has already developed a free searchable glossary with more than 1000 licensing terms, definitions, and uses. You can consult the glossary to find just the right words to use in a license agreement so that it will be easily understood by all parties. The online glossary can be found at: http://www.useplus. com/glossary.asp.

Use the PLUS glossary as a reference when creating licensing agreement. When licensing terminology is understood by both you and your clients, everybody wins.

Termination Rights for Copyright Licenses

Photographers often agree to bad deals early in their careers. Thanks to the Copyright Act, photographers may be able to minimize the damages resulting from those decisions.

Section 304(c) of the Copyright Act allows copyright owners (and their heirs) to terminate all grants, licenses or transfers of rights that were made prior to 1978 at the beginning of the 56th year after the grant (i.e., a license given in 1970 could be terminated in 2026). To terminate a transfer of rights, all requirements must strictly be met. The photographer must provide at least two years and no more than ten years' written notice to the licensee. The notice also must be filed with the U.S. Copyright Office. Similarly, grants, licenses or transfers made after 1977 may be terminated during the five-year period that begins 35 years after the grant was made.

The termination provisions do not apply to works for hire, so publishers and others who use photography are pushing to characterize future photographic assignments as works for hire. While you may agree to accept those terms, you should be sure that you completely understand the rights that you are giving away.

How Long Do You Own Your Copyright?

Copyrights don't last forever. In part, that's a good thing: now we can play Beethoven's Moonlight Sonata or take a photograph of Michelangelo's statue of David without paying royalties. When a work is not protected by copyright law, it is considered as being in the "public domain." The law is designed so that works of authorship eventually (or, in a few cases, immediately) are made available for all to benefit from and use freely.

Works go into public domain for one of three reasons:

(1) the author failed to satisfy the required statutory formalities needed to perfect the copyright;

(2) it is a work of the U.S. government; or

(3) the term of copyright has expired.

Item (1) only covers work published prior to March 1, 1989. At that time, the copyright notice had to be affixed to the work immediately or it immediately lost copyright protection. (Copyright protection has been restored for some foreign works even if they were published without notice before 1989.) That law has been changed; work published after 1989 does not need a copyright notice to maintain its copyright protection. It is, however, a good idea to use a copyright notice when displayed or offered in any manner.

                                        Photographer's Legal Guide

Item (2) refers to works created by government employees such as maps, charts, and surveys. They fall into the public domain from the date of creation.

Item (3) addresses the length of time that a work is protected by copyright law. Since the length of time that copyright protection remains in force has been changed several times over the years, it can be difficult to determine when exactly a given work falls into the public domain without doing some serious research. For photographs created after 1988, you (or your heirs) own the copyright for 70 years after your death (unless you have transferred it in writing). After that time, the copyright falls into the public domain; anyone can use the photos in any manner that they choose. For a period of time before 1988, copyrights expired 50 years after the copyright owner's death. Before then, the laws dealing with the length of copyright protection changed quite frequently. The chart found at http://www.unc.edu/~unclng/public-d.htm may be helpful in determining the applicable duration of copyrights for works established at various times.

Fortunately for photographers, the term of copyright protection is longer and easier to maintain than ever before. Do all that you can to protect your work.

Government Works Exception for Copyrights

Photographers often take pictures of statues and other artwork in national parks, such as the Lincoln Memorial, to sell as prints or postcards. Since the pieces of artwork are classified as works of the government, they are in the public domain; no permission is necessary to make a copy or to create a derivative work of them. But a little known provision called the "Government Works Exception" can get photographers into a lot of trouble.

Generally, copyright protection is not available for "any work of the United States Government." (17 U.S.C. Section 105.) Any work that is "prepared by an officer or employee of the United States Government as a part of that person's official duties" constitutes a "work of the United States Government." (17 U.S.C. Section 101.) Those works fall into the public domain.

Sometimes, however, copyrighted works are created by non-government personnel for the government, such as when the government commissions a piece of art. The artist later transfers the copyright to the government. The "government works exception" then allows the federal government to hold the copyrights for those works transferred to it by assignment. Some have argued that the government is using this exception unfairly as a way to circumvent the copyright law. The government works exception has been used to prevent the copying or creation of derivative works from such varied items as a film series on early Supreme Court cases and the Sacagawea coin.

The Vietnam Women's Memorial Foundation, Inc., ("VWMF") recently filed a lawsuit based on this exception against those who have sold photographs of the Vietnam Women's Memorial. The Memorial is a bronze sculpture created by Glenna Goodacre of Sante Fe. The sculpture resides on the grounds of the

Vietnam Veterans Memorial in Washington, D.C.; it depicts three women and a wounded soldier. Goodacre reportedly transferred the copyright of the sculpture to the VWMF. The VWMF is now suing various entities that allegedly sold photographs of the sculpture.

The VWMF claims copyright of the statue on its website. The VWMF could have avoided many unauthorized reproductions simply by placing a copyright notice on the statue, especially in view of the fact that the statue stands among government works that are in the public domain. How the VWMF case will turn out is hard to determine. It is always best to determine the copyright status of a creative work before photographing it.

The Copyright Notice

You'll often see a copyright "notice"—the familiar © or the word "copyright" with a date and name of the copyright owner—posted on creative works. A proper notice has three parts: the first part is the © (the letter "c" in a circle), the word "Copyright," or its abbreviation, "Copr." Some people use a "c" within parentheses like this: (c), but it has not been designated to be part of the official copyright notice. The second part notes the year when the work was first published. The third required part of a copyright notice is the name of the copyright owner. The final form looks like this: © 2007 Carolyn E. Wright. Including a copyright notice is no longer required for copyright protection, but it is a good idea to use it.

When you use the copyright notice it may stop someone from stealing your photographs, either because it serves as a reminder that the work is protected or because the notice interferes with the use of the work when it is part of the photo. Also, it helps to post a copyright notice on your photos because the infringer then cannot say the use was innocent. You may use the copyright notice without registering your work with the U.S. Copyright Office.

If you have a website that showcases your images, it is helpful to post a copyright notice on the pages of your website or when someone "right clicks" on your photos. Again, while the notice is not needed to protect the photos on your website or even the website itself, it can only help to use it. One caveat: you need to add the words "All Rights Reserved" so that your work is afforded additional protection in places such as South America.

Your basic notice should look like this: Copyright 2007 Carolyn E. Wright All Rights Reserved and should appear next to your photos wherever they are displayed. Or, you might choose to be more aggressive and use a notice like the one I use on my photography websites:

> All photographs appearing on this site are the property of Carolyn Wright Photography. They are protected by U.S. Copyright Laws and are not to be downloaded or reproduced in any way without the written permission of Carolyn Wright Photography. Copyright 2007 Carolyn E. Wright All Rights Reserved.

Feel free to copy and use this statement on your work (but don't forget to change the name).

Registering Your Copyrights

The Constitution gives Congress the power to enact laws establishing a system of copyright in the United States. Congress enacted the first federal copyright law in May 1790, and the first work was registered within two weeks. Today, the Copyright Office is a department of the Library of Congress. Claims to copyrights are registered at the Copyright Office. The Copyright Office also provides information about copyright law, guidelines for registering copyrights, and other valuable services.

Registration is not required to establish your copyrights or to use the copyright notice, but registration is necessary to file suit against an infringer. Properly registering your copyrights provides other benefits, as well. These benefits include:

- establishing a public record of the copyright;

- providing evidence of copyright ownership if registered within five years of publication;

- providing for statutory damages and attorney's fees if registered before infringement or within three months of publication; and

- preventing the importation of items that infringe on your copyright.

The owner of the copyright or the person with exclusive rights of the copyright (or an authorized agent of either of these persons, such as an attorney) may register a copyright. Registration is straightforward. For unpublished works, it merely requires that you file a copy of the photo(s) and the required forms with the U.S. Copyright Office. To register, send the following three items in the same envelope or package to the Library of Congress:

(1) a completed application form (use form VA for photographs;
(2) a non-refundable filing fee of $45 (check, money order or bank draft); and
(3) a non-returnable "deposit," which is a specific copy of the photos being registered.

The address is as follows:

Library of Congress
Copyright Office
101 Independence Avenue, S.E.,
Washington, D.C. 20559-6000

Step-by-step instructions for registering the copyrights of your images are included in the next section.

To make the registration process easier, your images may be registered as a collection with one application form and one fee. The images must be combined in an orderly format, the collection must have a single title, and the items in the collection must have the same copyright ownership. The current fee for registration is $45. If you register one image, the cost is $45. If you register a collection of a 1000 images, the fee is still $45.

The effective date of registration is the date that the Copyright Office receives the completed registration packet regardless of how long it takes the Office to process the registration. The Office will contact you if it has any questions and will send you a certificate after the registration has been processed. It will return any packages or items that are incomplete.

Steps to Register the Copyrights for Your Photographs

In this digital age, it is easier than ever for someone to steal your photographs. While the copyrights for your photographs are created at the click of the shutter, the best way to protect your photographs is to register them with the U.S. Copyright Office. In most cases, the required procedures to register your copyrights are easy. Follow the instructions carefully because mistakes in the process can limit your rights.

Even though the Copyright Office provides instructions to help you prepare the forms and gives information about copyright law on its website, the registration process can be daunting for some. The forms include lots of options, complex legal terms, and a variety of requirements. If, however, you are like the vast majority of photographers and no special circumstances are involved, the process of registering your photographs is fairly straightforward.

If you meet the following conditions, then the steps included below will help you register the copyrights for your photographs:

- The photos were taken by you, the photographer who is registering them.

- The photos were not taken in conjunction with a "work-for-hire" agreement. (See the definition of "work-for-hire" below.)

- You are a citizen of the United States.

- You have not previously registered the photographs.

- The photographs being registered are not collective or derivative works. (See the definitions below.)

- You do not have a "deposit account" with the U.S. Copyright Office. (If you have one, you would know it; if not, ignore this condition.)

- If you are registering previously "published" photographs, they must have been published in the United States after March 1, 1989. (See the definition of "publication" below.)

If you do not meet the conditions above, if there are any unusual circumstances or issues concerning your registrations, or if you wish to ensure the highest levels of protection, seek legal counsel to help register your copyrights. If you satisfy all of the conditions above, then follow the steps below to get started with the registration process.

Note: If you are registering a considerable number of published images, Form VA (as opposed to Short Form VA referenced below), may better fulfill your registration and legal needs.

Definitions

Following are definitions for some terms used when registering copyrights:

"Best edition" of published works — For our purposes, this refers to the best copy of your published photograph. Generally, when more than one version is available, the best edition is: larger rather than smaller; color rather than black and white; and printed on archival-quality rather than less permanent paper. For example, if your photo is published in an advertisement that is printed in a magazine and is posted on the web, then the page from the magazine showing your ad is the "best edition." If you post a photograph on your website and display that same photograph in a gallery, then the best edition is a digital file because that is the Copyright Office's preferred version for filing.

Compilation or Collective Works — A compilation or a collective work is formed when your photo is combined with other photos, text, illustrations, etc., to create a new work such as a book, a magazine, or a montage.

Complete Copy — For unpublished works, a complete copy is one that represents the complete copyrightable content of the work being registered, such as the entire photograph. For published works, it contains all elements of the publication, such as the entire photograph, the article with photographs, or the entire magazine, depending on the circumstances.

Derivative Work—A derivative work is one that is based on one or more earlier works. Derivative works include editorial revisions, annotations or other types of modifications. The work must be different enough from the original to be regarded as a new work—in other words, it must contain some substantial, not merely trivial, originality. The threshold for originality in a derivative work is higher than that required for the original work.

Publication—Publication is the distribution of copies of a photograph to the public by sale or other transfer of ownership, or by rental, lease, or lending; a work also is published if there has been an offering to distribute copies to a group of persons for purposes of further distribution or public display. Displaying a work, without doing anything else, does not constitute publication.

Work-for-Hire—The work-for-hire relationship is created in two situations: (1) when the photographer is an employee hired to photograph for the employer, such as a photojournalist who is an employee of a newspaper; or (2) the photographer is hired to provide photographs for collective works or compilations pursuant to a contract, and the contract specifically includes the provision that the copyrights to the images that are created for the contractor belong to the contractor.

Registration—Short Form VA

1. Download a copy of Short Form VA from the U.S. Copyright Office at http://www.copyright.gov/forms/formvas.pdf and prepare it as follows:
   a. Use a black pen or type your information on the registration form.
   b. Section 1
      i. Under "Title of This Work," create a descriptive title to reference the photograph(s) you are registering, such as "Alaska Trip 2006," or "All Published Photographs of Carolyn E. Wright in 2006."
      ii. For unpublished photographs, how you group your images is entirely up to you; be sure to keep the grouping logical.
      iii. Published photographs may be registered as one group if they were published in the same calendar year and were made by the same photographer. It's your decision if you want to register them in groups smaller than those published in one calendar year.
   c. Section 2
      i. Under "Name and Address..." put your name and address.
      ii. Include your nationality —"United States."
      iii. Your email, fax number and phone number are optional but it is a good idea to include them so that you can be contacted quickly if the Copyright Office has a question about your registration.
   d. Section 3
      i. For "Year of Creation," if registering a group of photographs, enter the year in which you took the most recent photograph.

e. Section 4
   i. If you are registering published works, under "Date and Nation of First Publication of This Particular Work," put the date or the range of dates that best indicate when the photographs in the group were published (such as March 12, 2006 or January—December 2006) and put "United States" for nation.
   ii. Leave this section blank if you are registering unpublished works.
f. Section 5
   i. For "Type of Authorship," check "Photograph."
g. Section 6
   i. Check the "Author" block and sign your name.
h. Section 7
   i. This section is optional, but is good to complete since it provides contact information in case someone outside the Copyright Office wants to contact you about your work.
   ii. If you select this option, check the box to indicate that the contact information is the same as that in Section 2.
i. Section 8
   i. Put your name and address where you want the registration certificate to be sent.
j. Section 9
   i. Ignore this section.

2. Prepare your photographs for deposit with the US Copyright Office.
   a. When registering unpublished photographs, send one copy of each photograph with the application.
   b. When registering published photographs, send two copies of the best edition of each photograph with the application.
   c. The copies will not be returned.
   d. You can send copies of the photos in the following formats (listed in the order of the Library of Congress' preference):
      i. Digital form on one or more CD-ROMs including CD-RWs and DVD-ROMs in one of these formats: jpeg, gif, tiff or pcd (an older format) (no minimum file size is required; while no maximum size is designated, a 100 pixel high or wide thumbnail that clearly depicts the photograph should be sufficient).
      ii. Unmounted prints at least 3 x 3 inches in size, but no larger than 20 x 24 inches.
      iii. Contact sheets.
      iv. Duplicate slides, each of a single image.
      v. A photocopy of each unmounted print at least 3 x 3 inches in size, but no larger than 20 x 24 inches.

vi. Slides, each containing a photograph of up to 36 images.

vii. A videotape clearly depicting each photograph.

3. Make a copy of all of your materials.

4. Send your materials in one package to:

    a. Library of Congress
Copyright Office
101 Independence Avenue, S.E.
Washington, D.C. 20559-6000

    b. Include:

        i. Completed Short Form VA.

        ii. Copies of your photographs prepared according to Section 2 above.

        iii. A check or money for the registration fee made payable to the Register of Copyrights. The fee is currently $45 per application.

    c. The suggested mailing method is via certified mail with a return receipt requested.

        i. Verified mailing service is not required.

        ii. It can take months to receive the certificate of registration. Since the registration is effective on the date it is received by the Copyright Office, you can better protect your rights if you can document the date your package is delivered.

    d. The suggested packaging to protect your items is a box not larger than 4" x 14" x 18."

Congratulations! You just completed a major step towards protecting your work!

"Copyrighting" vs. "Registering" Your Photos

Many photographers have learned the advantages of sending copies of their photos along with the required VA form and check to the U.S. Copyright Office. By doing so, you are registering your copyrights. Some call this "copyrighting" their photos, but that term is not technically correct and using it may cause problems. Copyrights for photographers are created at the click of the shutter—it does not matter whether an image was recorded on film or by digital methods. Once the image is created, the laws that relate to the copyright of that image are effective immediately. Even if the photograph is never registered, the copyright exists and is protected by copyright law.

If the copyright is later registered, additional benefits arise, such as the option to recover statutory damages for infringements and the inference that the person who registered the copyright is the owner.

If photographers tell others that they are "copyrighting" their photos when they actually are registering them, others may believe that the photos are not protected until that time. Some may feel free to use the photos without permission or may not give photographers their due credit.

To best protect your work, "register" your copyrights as soon as you can (and refer to it that way).

Registering the Copyrights of Published Works

Copyright registration requirements are different for copyrights of works that have been "published" previously. According to the U.S. Copyright Office, you have published your work when you distribute copies of it to the public by sale, lending, or leasing. Publication also includes the offering to distribute copies of your work to others for the purpose of further distribution. Simply displaying a work does not in and of itself constitute publication.

Does Posting Photos on Website = Publishing?

Many photographers post their images on the web. Are those images "published" for purposes of copyright registration? It depends.

The courts have not spoken directly as to whether posting a photo on a website constitutes publication. The courts have ruled that displaying but not selling photos in a gallery did not constitute a publication of the photos. Therefore, it most likely is dependent on how and where the work is posted on the web that will dictate whether the photos have been published. In other words, it is not the act of posting a photograph on a website but the intent of the posting that determines whether or not a photo is published.

If you are offering to license the image or sell a print of the photo from your website, it likely would be classified as having been published. If you are posting an image only to share with others without any obvious intent to sell or further distribute it, it will most likely be deemed to have not been published. Posting an image on a forum such as NatureScapes.net for critique or posting images in a password-protected area probably does not meet that threshold.

If you are not sure whether a photo has been published, then you most likely should register it as published. It may not hurt you to register an image as published even if it is later determined not to have been published (but for the extra registration work involved). It can hurt you to register an image as unpublished if it is later deemed to have been published. If you register a photo incorrectly as unpublished, your registration may be deemed invalid because the deposit requirements are different for published works.

Bulk Registration of Published Images

There's no doubt that it's easier to register your photographs before you publish them. But if you didn't do it then, it's better late than never to register your published images. The good news is that it's more convenient and cheaper now to register your photographs after they have been published than it has ever been before.

Pursuant to a recent change in copyright law, you now can register a group of published images on one form. The only requirements are that:

- The photographs were made by the same photographer (or are owned by an employer in a work-for-hire situation);

- The photographs were published in the same calendar year; and

- The photographs have the same copyright claimant.

Because you must identify the title, date of publication, and nation of publication for each published photograph you register, you may use Form GR/PPh/Con (Group Registration of Published Photographs Continuation Form) to record that information with your deposit. The Form also has a place to describe each photo, but that is optional. Since deposits (such as prints, CDs, and slides) can degrade with time, the description will assist with identifying the work you have registered.

Previously, there was no limit to the number of photographs that you could include in a group registration of published images. But think of the poor U.S. Copyright Office employee who opened a recent registration package that consisted of a staggering total of 1,776 Continuation Forms! It's no wonder that the Copyright Office quickly amended its regulations to limit the number of photographs that may be submitted with a single application form and filing fee to 750 (that would require 50 forms).

There still is no limit to the number of photographs that may be included in a single group registration of published images when you elect not to use Continuation Forms. You can, instead, identify the title, date of publication, and nation of publication for each photograph in a text file on the CD-ROM or DVD that contains the photographic images or include a separate list that provides the same information for each image.

You no longer have an excuse: go to the dentist, change the oil in your car, and register your images, both unpublished and published. It's better late than never.

Registering Your Website

Many photographers design websites so that they can share their images. If the design of your website meets a standard of originality, it is subject to copyright protection just as your photographs are. The bonus is that when you register your website, you also can register the photos and text on your website on one form and with one fee to protect all of your work.

   Photographer's Legal Guide

Registering your website covers the copyrightable content of the website as identified in your registration. You should specifically exclude any material that has been previously registered, was published in an earlier calendar year, or is in the public domain. For newly published works, limit your registration to the content of the work that is published on the date given on the application.

To register, use the form that corresponds to the type of authorship being registered, for example:

> Form TX - literary material, including computer programs and databases
>
> Form VA - pictorial and graphic works, including cartographic material
>
> Form PA - audiovisual material, including any sounds, music, or lyrics

If the work contains more than one type of authorship, use the form that corresponds to the predominant material. For registering computer programs with text and photos, Form TX is likely the best form. There, Section 5 TX asks for:

> Type of Authorship in This Work
>
> - Text (includes fiction, nonfiction, poetry, computer programs, etc.)
> - Illustrations
> - Photographs
> - Compilation of terms or data

You may check one, more, or all of the boxes on the same form. More information is available on the Copyright Office's website at www.copyright.gov in Circular #66.

You'll need to register your website each time that you post new photographs or text or after making changes to the website that constitute original work. Use a new application form and pay a separate filing fee for each subsequent registration.

Protecting your work as a photographer often goes beyond the pictures that you create. Do what is necessary to protect all of it.

Correcting Copyright Registration Mistakes

Registering your copyrights with the U.S. Copyright Office is undoubtedly important. It gives you the legal presumption that the work is yours, the right to elect statutory damages for subsequent infringements, and the right to file suit to prosecute those who infringe your copyrights. But you must follow specific instructions when registering your photographs to ensure the most complete protection.

Congratulations are in order if you already have registered your photos, but what happens if you later realize that you made an error on the registration? Is the registration valid? It depends.

In general, a copyright may be registered only once. When you register your copyright, bits of information are collected about the work. The principal uses of that information are to establish and maintain a public record and to determine whether the registration complies with copyright law. Other uses include public inspection and copying and preparation of public indexes and catalogs.

If you later discover that the registration for a photograph is incorrect or incomplete, you may file a supplementary registration, also known as Form CA; use this form to correct an error or to augment the previous information. The photographer, another person owning the copyright, or an agent for either of those persons may file the supplemental registration.

Form CA should be used only for errors or omissions on the initial registration —not for other changes to the original registration. For example, do not file a supplemental registration to document a change in the work. Significant modifications become derivative works entitled to their separate registrations. Do not use Form CA when a work that you previously registered as unpublished is later published or when you transfer the copyright.

When you file a supplemental registration, the work is assigned a new number; your rights may be affected. The best thing to do is to file the initial registration accurately.

Safeguards for Collective Works

Photographers often submit photos to publishers for inclusion in a book or magazine; what happens to the copyright for that photo? Does it transfer to the publisher? If so, what is the publisher allowed to do with the copyright?

Unless the copyright to a photo is specifically transferred in total and in writing to a publisher, the publisher's use of that photo is limited by the usage agreement. When your photo is combined with other photos, text, illustrations, etc., the publisher has created a new copyright-able work called a "collective work." Your photo then is protected by two copyrights —one for the photo itself, and the other as part of a collective work.

As the owner of the copyright of a collective work, the publisher may reproduce and distribute your contribution as part of that particular collective work, but not as a separate item. The publisher also may distribute any "revision" of that collective work in a later collective work as long as it is part of the same series. A "revision" may be thought of as a new version that is still considered to be one work.

                                    Photographer's Legal Guide

Revision became an issue with some photographers who had contributed work to National Geographic magazine. National Geographic distributed CDs that included previously published magazine issues almost exactly as they appeared in print. National Geographic added a search engine and an index to the CDs. The photographers argued that this constituted a new use of their images and wanted to be paid for it. National Geographic argued that the CDs were a revision of the collective work (the magazines) so that the usage was included in the initial grant of rights. Because the photographers were located in different parts of the United States, they filed their lawsuits in two separate courts. Both cases were appealed. The 2nd and 11th Circuit Courts of Appeal came to different conclusions as to whether the CDs were a revision or a new product. This inconsistency in the law may have to be resolved in the future.

While hindsight is 20-20, we can learn from this experience that the best way to protect your copyrights is to be as specific as possible when granting usage rights. If you don't want your photos used for certain purposes, say so. But if your license doesn't address a specific usage, the court that might not agree with your position just may be the one that decides your case.

The Publisher's Copyright Registration Is Not Enough

Photographers often publish photos along with other images and/or text in magazines, books, calendars, etc. While the publishers of those "collective works" are quick to register the copyright for the collective work, photographers sometimes are not as diligent. Does the publisher's copyright protect the photographer's image as well as the magazine?

Section 101 of the Copyright Act defines a collective work as "a work, such as a periodical issue, anthology, or encyclopedia, in which a number of contributions, constituting separate and independent works, are assembled into a collective whole." A collective work is a type of "compilation." Section 103 defines a compilation as copyrightable subject matter. It is a "work formed by the collection and assembling of preexisting materials or of data that are selected, coordinated, or arranged in such a way that the resulting work as a whole constitutes an original work of authorship." It is not necessary that the contributions come from different authors or photographers to comprise a compilation, but they often do.

As with magazines or books, a collective work may be registered and the registration protects all of the copyrightable elements that comprise the collective work. That is, the specific selection, coordination, or arrangement of the individual works that make up the entire work is protected.

However, a publisher's copyright registration extends only to the compilation —not to the individual works that make up that compilation unless the publisher also owns the copyrights to those works.

If your photograph is part of a collective work or a compilation, don't rely on the publisher's copyright registration to protect your work; it won't. Register the copyright yourself.

Honoring the Copyrights of Others

Using Music To Enhance Your Photos

When presenting public programs, many photographers use music to enhance their photography. But since music is a work protected by copyright law, they must be sure to honor the copyright of the composer.

Most photographers recognize that copying music from a friend or downloading from a music sharing website is illegal, but even if you purchased the CD or song outright, you may be infringing on the copyrights if you use the music for more than personal purposes.

When you buy music, you are not purchasing the copyright; you are getting a license to use the music in specific ways (just as when you license an image to a company for a specific use). If the company uses your image beyond the established permissions, your copyright is infringed. If you give a bride copies of the photos from her wedding and inform her that they are for personal use only, she would violate your copyright even if she donated them to "Bride's Magazine."

In general, when you buy a CD or a song, you are permitted personal use only. If you play the music during a party at your house, you probably are still using the music within the particular boundaries. But if you play the music in your commercial studio or use it to accompany your slideshow presentation for a client, you more than likely have gone beyond the rights granted to you when you purchased the CD. Check the small print on the CD to be sure.

What are your options if you want some music for your photography? You can write your own music, get permission directly from the composer, or license it from authorized agencies—ACSAP (www.ascap.com), BMI (www.bmi.com), or SESAC (www.sesac.com). There are some websites that make it easier to obtain those rights, such as www.musicbakery.com or www.freeplaymusic.com. You can use software such as Apple's new Soundtrack Pro or Garage Band to create your own music. These programs are easy to use even if you don't have much musical skill.

Just as photographers don't want their copyrights infringed, composers don't either. Respect a composer's work. Get the necessary license or permission when using music to support your photography.

Photographing Other Copyrighted Items

Photographers often photograph sculptures in parks or other publicly accessible areas. While sculptors have difficulty preventing all unauthorized reproductions of their copyrighted works, it can be worth their while to prosecute those who make money off of those reproductions.

Take, for example, the famous bull sculpture that has come to symbolize Wall Street. It took the sculptor, Arturo Di Modica, two years and $350,000 to create the bull. He originally placed it in front of the New York Stock Exchange but the police had it moved to Bowling Green Park.

Modica registered the bull sculpture in 1998. As the copyright owner, he has the exclusive right:

    · To reproduce the copyrighted work;
    · To display the copyrighted work publicly;
    · To prepare derivative works based on the copyrighted work; and
    · To distribute copies of the copyrighted work to the public by sale, by renting or lending, and/or by displaying the image.

Arturo has made money from display of the bull in movies and advertising. But he recently filed suit against Wal-Mart, several galleries, and others for selling photos and reproductions of the bull without his permission. He has asked that the alleged infringers cease and desist their activities and to pay him a share of their profits.

Arturo's litigation is still in the courts. In the meantime, be sure to get permission from copyright owners before photographing their work; if not, they may first see red and then green.

International Protection for Your Copyrights

There is no international protection for copyrights. Some countries, however, as members of the Berne Convention, will give certain copyright protection for photographs under specific conditions. Additional information is available from the U.S. Copyright Office's Circular 38a (entitled, "International Copyright Relations of the United States"). Some additional protection for images may be afforded in some countries by adding the words "All Rights Reserved" to your copyright notice.

Copyright Protection for Foreign Photographers

Copyright law in the United States is relatively favorable for photographers, both for U.S. residents and those abroad. All unpublished photos, regardless of where they were made or by whom they were made, are protected in the United States. Any photo that is protected by U.S. copyright law can be registered; that includes works of foreign origin. When using Short Form VA for registering photographs, section 2 asks for your name, address, and your nationality or domicile (the country that you consider your "home"). It does not require that you be a U.S. citizen.

If your photos are first published in the United States or in a country with which the U.S. has a copyright treaty, they are protected and may therefore be registered with the U.S. Copyright Office. Also, if you are a citizen of or reside in a country that has a copyright treaty with the U.S., then you can register your photos with the U.S. Copyright Office. See Circular 38a, International Copyright Relations of the United States, for a list of countries that have a copyright treaty with the U.S.

If you are a foreigner who registers your images with the U.S. Copyright Office, you will likely find it worth the time and effort to prosecute infringements that occur in the United States. Foreign photographers, register your images in the U.S. now!

Protection for Your Derivative Works

Here's the issue: you photograph a car for the manufacturer in 2006 and register the photo with U.S. Copyright Office. In 2007, the car-maker produces the same car with a different style of wheels. The client asks you to shoot only the new wheels and add them to the original photo using Photoshop. The new photo then will be distributed. Do you need to register the new photograph to obtain full copyright protection? You do if it would qualify as a derivative work.

As the owner of a copyright, you have complete and exclusive control of your photograph; you and only you have the right to prepare derivative works based on the original image. But when you alter a work, it is a judgment call as to whether the result constitutes a derivative work or is a minor variation of the original work.

A derivative work is one that is based on one or more earlier works. Derivative works include editorial revisions, annotations, or other modifications. A derivative work must be different enough from the original to be regarded a new work—in other words, it must contain some substantial, not merely trivial, originality. Making minor changes or additions of little substance to a preexisting work will not make it a new version for copyright purposes.

One of the tests for deciding if a new work is a derivative work is to consider whether the new material is original and copyrightable in and of itself. Note, for reasons not covered here, that the standard of originality is higher for derivative works than it is for those that are not based on preexisting works.

If your photo meets the definition of a derivative work, the copyright must be registered to ensure full statutory protection. If the photo is only slightly modified and does not qualify as a derivative work, then the original copyright registration covers the work.

In the case cited above, the photograph of the wheels would be considered original and copyrightable itself; adding it to the original photograph would pretty

                                    Photographer's Legal Guide

much ensure that it would be ruled a new work. Be safe: for the utmost protection, register the new work.

How to Prevent Others from Stealing Your Photos

Software companies have recently been getting more aggressive in pursuing infringers of their software. Should this matter to you? Photographers do not want their intellectual property—copyrights or trademarks—stolen. When we share a music CD or a pirated copy of Photoshop with a friend, we are doing unto others what we do not want done to us. We are perpetuating the problem of copyright infringement, even if on a small scale. Is it OK to steal a pack of gum but not a car?

Here's what you can do to keep people from stealing your images. First, don't steal the work of others. Stop the cycle.

Next, educate the infringers. Some people don't realize that playing music from a CD in a commercial setting or downloading a photo to use as a screensaver is illegal. To combat this, the Business Software Alliance has developed programs to promote an understanding of copyright protection and cyber security for trade and e-commerce. BSA's members include software industry giants such as Adobe and Microsoft.

BSA apparently recognizes that the best way to fight infringement is to raise people's awareness of it at an early age. BSA has created a comic book called "Copyright Crusader to the Rescue." It was developed to teach children about cyber ethics, including responsible computer and Internet use, respect for digital creativity, and copyright protection.

The recording industry also has increased its public awareness program and found a significant rise in the percentage of persons aware that it is illegal to make copyrighted music available online for others to download. When some people know that an activity is illegal, they don't do it.

Third, we can develop and use the existing technology that makes it difficult for others to steal our work. Some thieves are lazy and won't attempt to do so if it takes much effort. Put watermarks on your images. This function puts the copyright notice directly on the photo so that unauthorized use is impaired and the viewer is put on notice of copyright protection. Include your web address or other contact information in the watermark for the convenience of potential customers.

Fourth, help your customers to understand exactly what they can do with your photos. Include a delivery memo with your photos that documents what you are sending. Be sure to identify specifically and in writing the limited rights that you are granting to a user. And make sure to put your copyright notice on all of your work.

Fifth, make it easier for potential infringers to purchase the product that they might otherwise be tempted to steal. The recording industry has learned that consumers will readily purchase one song when they are reluctant to buy an entire album. Be willing to modify your licenses to meet the client's needs. Include your name and your contact info with the images, including in the metadata.

Last, we can enforce our copyrights by suing those who steal our photos so that they and others will learn that the theft will not be tolerated. Send the message that it's not OK to steal either the gum or the car.

Additional Ways to Protect Your Photos

While you will never be able to prevent all unauthorized uses of your photos, there are additional ways to protect them. A bit of preparation can prevent many of those attempts to infringe.

Photographers often post their images on websites or send digital copies to clients and friends. Those photos can be easily copied and forwarded to others. If copyright information is not included with the photos, it can result in the loss of sales, the loss of willful infringement damages, and/or the loss of credit for the work. Fortunately, there are good ways to provide your important contact and copyright information with your photos.

Adobe Photoshop, Aperture, and other photo editing and cataloging programs allow you to embed your copyright and contact information in the metadata of the photo file. After you have opened an image in Photoshop, select File, and then File Info, and then enter the copyright information there. The other editing and cataloging programs work similarly. Note that this metadata will be removed by using the "Save for Web" utility.

Additional ways to protect your photos includes tracking your photos on the web with programs like "Digimarc" (www.digimarc.com) to find unauthorized uses, blocking "right clicking" on web photos, and reducing the file sizes of your photos on the Internet so that it is more difficult to reproduce your photos in print materials. While sophisticated computer users can override your efforts to protect your work, making it more difficult to steal your photos will thwart many unauthorized uses. Although infringements will never be stopped, photographers should do what they can to prevent them.

Protecting Your Copyrights and Prosecuting Infringers

When your image is used without your permission, your copyright is infringed. You have several options at this point.

- You can do nothing. You may not care that a non-profit wolf society is using one of your wolf images on its web site.

  Photographer's Legal Guide

- You may want only proper credit for the use of the photo. If so, write the society a letter granting it the right to use the image (be sure to designate the parameters of that usage), but insist that you get a photo credit that includes a copyright notice. Also ask the society to add your name and an active link to your website. This may generate additional work from the society or from others.

- You may want the infringer to stop using your image. Send the infringer a "cease and desist" letter. It carries more weight if the letter comes from an attorney.

- You also can demand that the infringer pay you for the use. The amount of the demand can range from what you would have charged if the infringer had paid for use of the image in the first place to the amount of money you believe is due to you for the infringement. If the infringer agrees to pay the latter amount, that will avoid attorney's fees for both sides and will allow you to be paid more quickly. (Note: Many photographers ask for three (3) times the normal licensee fee for infringements but there is no legal basis for this.) If the infringers are business-savvy, they will know that they are in trouble. If they do not understand the dire consequences of infringements, they will as soon as they get a chance to speak with their attorney. They will want to avoid the legal fees that will be imposed both by their and your attorney. The import of your demand letter is dramatically increased if it comes from an attorney. The infringer will recognize that you mean business and are prepared to go forward with a lawsuit if the infringer doesn't respond appropriately.

- You can pursue remedies pursuant to the Digital Millennium Copyright Act (see below).

- Your most aggressive option is to pursue your legal remedies by filing suit. Remember, your copyright must first be registered with the Copyright Office if you wish to file an infringement case. You must file the lawsuit in federal court. An option would be to file a breach of contract claim in state court (see below for specifics). Get an attorney to help you because the legal procedures involved are quite complicated.

Protecting your copyrights and prosecuting the infringers go hand in hand. When it comes to protecting your rights, what you do after your copyright is infringed is at least as important as what you do beforehand.

Filing Suit for Copyright Infringement or Breach of Contract

Many copyright infringements arise when clients use your image beyond what is legally permitted by the license that is in place. Other infringements arise when the client neglects to pay your invoice in part or full. In either case, the good news is that there are several options open to you. You may sue in federal court for infringement after registering your copyright with the U.S. Copyright Office or you may sue in state court for breach of contract.

Take, for example, the case of Effects Associates ["EA"] vs. Cohen from the 9th Circuit Court of Appeals. Cohen verbally hired EA to prepare film footage. Cohen paid EA only half of the agreed amount because he was not completely satisfied with the footage. He did, however, use the footage anyway. EA sued Cohen for copyright infringement. Although Cohen had not paid EA in full for the use, the court held that EA had granted Cohen an "implied" license to use the film footage. Although it dismissed the infringement case, the court noted that EA could sue Cohen in state court on a breach of contract claim for not paying for the license.

We can learn several things from this case. First, always put your licenses in writing. You don't want the court to decide what you meant to do. As the court in the EA case explained, "[putting agreements in writing] prevents misunderstandings by spelling out the terms of a deal in black and white, forces parties to clarify their thinking and consider problems that could potentially arise, and encourages them to take their promises seriously because it's harder to backtrack on a written contract than on an oral one."

Second, make your licenses subject to being paid in full. This language can include: "Until we have agreed to the terms under which you will use [the work] and have paid me the agreed-upon fee, you have no rights to make any use of this work. Any unauthorized use constitutes willful infringement." Without those conditions, you may forego your right to pursue an infringement claim when you have not been paid for your work.

Finally, as a copyright holder, you are the "master of your claim;" you can opt to pursue copyright infringement or breach of contract whenever someone uses your work without permission. The facts of the case may dictate which option is best for recovery. An attorney can help you make that decision. Whatever you do, take some action to protect your work.

What to Do When Minors Infringe

Some of the most technically astute people these days are the young. Many can disable sophisticated protection devices and then copy your photos from the web. They are wizards at using photo-editing programs to make impressive derivative works or prints from up-rezzed files copied off of the Internet. Can you sue minors for those infringements? It depends.

As noted in the contracts chapter, minors don't have the capacity to contract. But you may be able to sue them. While copyright infringement cases are filed in federal court, federal courts will look to the state law where the minors live to determine whether you can hold them responsible for their infringements. The courts will usually appoint guardians to represent the minors.

While you may not want to prosecute little Susie for using your photo of a koala bear as her screen saver, you may get a little peeved when you find little Johnny selling t-shirts emblazoned with a silk-screen copy of your best grizzly image.

Digital Millennium Copyright Act

The Digital Millennium Copyright Act (DMCA), enacted in 1998, implemented treaties signed at the 1996 World Intellectual Property Organization (WIPO) Geneva conference. It addresses many issues, one of which affects photographers directly. The DMCA states that while an Internet Service Provider (ISP) is not liable for transmitting information that may infringe a copyright, the ISP must remove materials from users' websites that appear to constitute copyright infringement.

Your copyright does not have to be registered with the U.S. Copyright Office for you to take advantage of these provisions and the protection that they provide. If you find a website that is using one of your images without permission, contact the hosting ISP and report the infringement. The ISP is required to make its agent's name and address available so that you can send them notification.

When you notify the ISP of infringement, it must meet certain requirements. The notification must:

- Be in writing;

- Be signed by the copyright owner or agent; your electronic signature is OK;

- Identify the copyrighted work that you claim has been infringed (or a list of infringements from the same site);

- Identify the material that is infringing your work;

- Include your contact info;

- State that you are complaining in "good faith;"

- State that, "under penalty of perjury, that the information contained in the notification is accurate;" and

- State that you have the right to proceed (because you are the copyright owner or the owner's agent).

After the ISP receives the notice, it should remove the infringing materials.

The DMCA also provides for certain damages when your work is infringed. If the infringer has removed your copyright notice from your work in an attempt to facilitate or conceal its infringement, the infringer may have violated the DMCA. Section 1202(b) of the DMCA prohibits the removal of "copyright management information" in certain circumstances. It states in pertinent part:

> No person shall, without the authority of the copyright owner or the law—(1) intentionally remove or alter any copyright management information . . . . knowing, or, with respect to civil remedies . . . having reasonable grounds to know, that it will induce, enable, facilitate, or conceal an infringement of any right under this title.

The statutory award for each violation of Section 1202 ranges from $2,500 to $25,000. The DMCA is another important tool in the photographer's legal toolkit.

Award Money for Infringements

Do not be too distressed if someone steals your copyrighted image. In many cases, it can be more profitable if they do so; you can often make more money from copyright enforcement than you can from selling the image. Many photographers overreact to the fear of having their images stolen that it limits the distribution of their images. As long as you follow the suggestions provided in this book, you will be protected in one way or another.

When your copyright is infringed, you may make a claim for the actual profits earned by the infringer that are the direct result of the infringement. It can be difficult to prove the exact amount but the award can be significant depending on the circumstances. One photographer recently settled with the Dallas Cowboys for almost $300,000. The Cowboys had used one of his images on items of clothing and other merchandise without his permission.

The photographer had given a digital file of a photograph to the Cowboys who considered it for use on season tickets. The Cowboys then bought the rights to market 250 prints to the public. Later, the Cowboys used the same image on clothing and other items without getting permission from the photographer for the additional usage.

Because the photographer had not registered his photo with the U.S. Copyright Office prior to the infringement, he could seek only actual damages—essentially the licensing fee he would have charge for the authorized use plus the profits earned by the Cowboys as a result of the infringement. Had he registered the

Photographer's Legal Guide

image prior to the infringement, he would have been eligible for statutory damages up to $150,000 per infringing use.

When the photographer discovered the infringements and inquired about them, the Cowboys offered him $1,000 in merchandise gift certificates. After trying to negotiate a settlement on his own for about a year, he hired a lawyer. Three years later, the settlement was reached.

Morals of the story:

- Many infringements come from uses beyond those agreed to. The infringements can come from uses on different products, for longer terms, in extra formats such as print or electronic, in other locations, etc. Keep your eye on your client's use of your work.

- Register your images with the U.S. Copyright Office before or within three months of giving them to a client.

- Even if you haven't registered your photographs with the U.S. Copyright Office, you are entitled to the actual damages as determined by the profits obtained by the infringer as a result of the infringement. Though the exact amount can be hard to prove, the awards can be quite substantial.

- While you may be a good negotiator, it can help to have a lawyer to give weight to your position and to advise you on your rights.

- Legal matters can take time; be patient.

If the timing of your copyright registration is proper, you may elect to seek statutory damages instead of the actual profits of the infringer. Statutory fees can range from $750 to $30,000 per infringement (the range for the statutory fees is what the court believes is necessary to deter the infringer from future infringements), and up to $150,000 with attorney's fees if the infringement was willful or intentional. Statutory fees usually amount to much more than actual profits.

What is "proper" timing for registration? At a minimum, it should be anytime before the infringement occurs. Your registration is effective the day it is received by the U.S. Copyright Office, so be sure to send your registration materials via a documented delivery method.

You also are eligible for statutory fees as long as you register your copyright within three months of it being published. If your photo is infringed even one day after it is published but your registration reaches the U.S. Copyright Office three-months-minus-one-day later, you will be protected. Basically, the three months is a grace period that may allow photographers to get their ducks in a row.

If your photograph has been infringed, you have not registered it, and it is more than three months since you published it, register it as soon as you can for two reasons. First, you must register your photo to file suit in court. Second, if one infringer found the image worth stealing, it is likely that another will, too.

The Statute of Limitations for Copyrights

When someone infringes your copyright, the time that you have to make your claim is limited. This is based on a legal principle called "the statute of limitations." Statutes of limitation, in general, are laws that prescribe the time limits during which you can file lawsuits. The deadlines vary with the type of claim and—at times—they depend on the state where you live. The purpose of them is to reduce the unfairness of defending actions after a substantial period of time has elapsed. They allow people to go on with their lives, regardless of guilt, after a certain amount of time has passed.

Because copyrights are governed by federal law, there is only one statute of limitations for copyright-related claims. Copyright infringement claims have a three-year statute of limitations from the date of the "last act" of the infringement. What constitutes the last act can vary. If your image is published in a newspaper without your permission, you have three years from the date that the newspaper was distributed to file your claim in court. If the infringement continues, such as when someone is using your image on the web without your consent, the clock would begin to run only when your photo is removed from the website. Determining when a statute of limitation has started to run can be a bit tricky. It may begin when you have "constructive" notice of the infringement; that is, you should have known about the infringement, even if you didn't have actual knowledge of it. An example of constructive notice is when your photo is published in a nationally-distributed magazine but you don't see a copy of it.

If someone uses your photo without your permission, you may seek legal remedy from that person within three years of the last act of infringement. Do not sit on a claim once you have it. Note, however, that in all cases you must first register your copyright with the U.S. Copyright Office if you wish to pursue any copyright infringement claims in court.

Estate Planning for your Copyrights

Photographers may think that their most important property items are their expensive digital SLR and lenses. But their copyrights last much longer and can be more valuable. Sadly, photographers rarely protect and manage their copyrights as well as they do their equipment, including in their estate planning. Fortunately, there is an easy way to correct that deficiency.

Copyrights are one form of intellectual property ("IP"). IP rights may be protected at law in the same way as any other form of property, such as your house, car and camera equipment. Because copyrights created since 1978 last 70 years after the photographer's death, they can have significant value. If you include them in your will, you can direct their use after you're gone.   Otherwise, they will be passed along as personal property according to state law.

Recently, a famous book author failed to plan for the management of his copyright upon his death. After hearing of the situation, a concerned lawyer prepared a simple will that may help creatives, including photographers, to more easily make plans for their IP after their death. The details are available at www.neilgaiman.com.

If the value of your copyrights is significant, the estate taxes that will be incurred by the inheriting party can be exorbitant. Seek counsel from a good tax lawyer to reduce those tax liabilities as much as possible.

Not to decide to protect your work is to decide that your work won't be protected. Do what you can today to make sure that your heirs benefit from your hard work and talent.

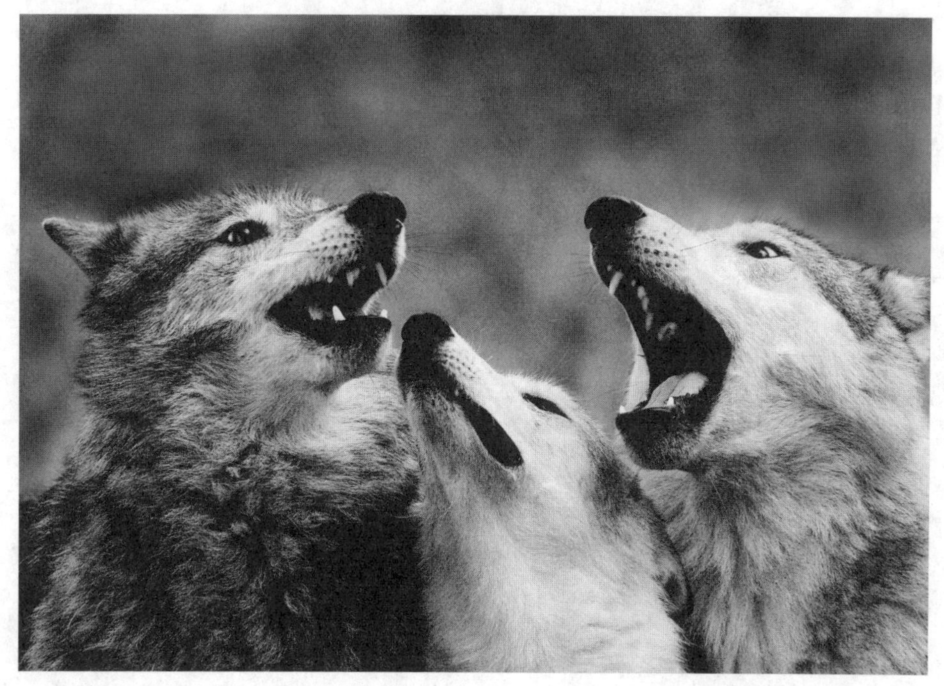

Photographer's Legal Guide

Contracts For Your Photography Business

What is a Contract?

Most hobbyist and all professional photographers need to use contracts to protect themselves and their business. A contract is a legally enforceable agreement entered into by the parties: you and a client, customer, or anyone else who wants to make an agreement with you. Each of the parties to the contract consents to do (or not do) something in exchange for something else. A contract requires a meeting of the minds or "mutual assent." It comes about by an offer and an acceptance. Every contract must have "consideration," which means that all parties agree to give up or to do something. If that "something" is not clear, disagreements arise. So be as specific as you can about what it is you are agreeing to do to save yourself from later problems.

You cannot enter a contract that requires a party to do something that is illegal or contrary to public policy. It would be void as a matter of law.

Every transaction, whether it's with a vendor or a client, should be based on a contract. While a contract may be created orally, it benefits all parties to have a written contract so that the obligations and benefits are clear to all. While the parties to the contract may subsequently disagree about what that contract means, putting it in writing should make your agreement clearer.

The contract doesn't have to be a formal document drafted by a lawyer. While a lawyer is trained to help you anticipate and thus prevent problems, contracts such as the one that was written on a restaurant napkin between non-lawyers have been enforced.

Contracts in Electronic Form

A contract may be in any memorandum form, including electronic mail. It is "signed" by any mark, written, stamped or engraved, which demonstrates the intent to agree to the contract. With the prevalence of email and web-based solicitations, this can be a concern for photographers.

For example, an airline company recently sponsored a contest. The grand prize was a year's worth of flying, and most anyone could use that. You entered by submitting a photo, an essay or a video. On the contest's website, you were directed to the page titled, "Legal Terms and Conditions." You had to scan down to read the entire text. While most folks might "accept" the terms without reading them, the fine print on this page has some information that was of the utmost importance that a photographer should read. The terms stated in part:

> For good and valuable consideration . . . I hereby assign and
> transfer in perpetuity to [the airline company] . . . all world-wide
> rights, title, and interest in . . . to all: . . . photographs . . . copy-
> rights (including the right to register the copyright and any re-
> newals or reversions thereof) . . . derivative works, and any other
> material and/or intellectual property embodied in the material
> created and submitted by me [for the contest].

If you had agreed to this, you would have just transferred (rather than licensed) your copyright to the airlines, regardless of whether you won a prize. Once you had transferred your copyright, it would have given the airlines all rights to the photograph (as if the airlines had taken it).

Similar events are occurring elsewhere. The license for an instant messaging product gives the company

> [A]ll right, title and interest in any compilation, collective work
> or other derivative work created by [the company] using or
> incorporating [the] . . . content. You grant [the company] . . . the
> irrevocable, perpetual worldwide rights to reproduce, display . . .
> this content . . . ."

This gives the company a license to use any photo transmitted while using its instant messenger service. In the company's defense, such a license may be necessary to protect the company from copyright infringement suits concerning images transmitted by the service. On the contrary, a transfer of copyright is not necessary for an airline company to run its contest.

Since you can "sign" a document by responding electronically, be very careful when answering emails or when responding to website solicitations. Always read the fine print to protect your copyrights.

Capacity to Contract

Photographers often enter into contracts with others, especially when hired to do a shoot. But if the client does not have capacity to contract, then the contract might not be worth the paper it's written on. You may get stuck doing the job for free.

While people generally are given the freedom to contract, they sometimes are deemed by law to be unable to make decisions in their best interest. The law believes that minors, people with a mental disability, those who are in bankruptcy, or people who have impaired judgment due to illness, disability, hypnosis, alcohol or drug use, do not have capacity to contract. While you may agree to photograph a bride's wedding and she promises to pay you, she can later disaffirm that contract if she is a minor (under 18 for most states). If you already have shot the wedding when she voids the contract, you may not be paid.

                                        Photographer's Legal Guide

The test of whether someone was mentally impaired when contracting is if he could understand the nature and effect of the contract. Contracts with mentally impaired are void only when a court has previously determined the person to be mentally incompetent.

When contracting with clients, make sure that when they sign on the dotted line they have the capacity to be bound to that contract.

Other Tips for Contracts

While you should hold onto the original, signed contract for your files, the other party may keep a copy as a record. If you don't have a copy machine, you and the other party can sign a copy of the contract and note on the contract that it is a "conformed copy." Make sure that all of the contract provisions in the copy are the same as in the original.

So whether you hire a lawyer, use a form, or just use your best judgment as to what to include in the contract, get it in writing. It's better than trying to remember what you each agreed to do. Putting the terms of the agreement in writing also makes a contract enforceable for up to six years (depending on the type of contract and the place where the contract was made) rather than one year, due to a legal restriction called the "statute of frauds." Also, some contracts must be in writing to be enforceable. Contracts relating to the sale of goods or services more than a year in advance (such as when you agree to photograph a wedding that is more than a year away) would fit this group.

Clients sometimes display discomfort when signing contracts. In response, photographers may try to explain what the contract says so that it doesn't seem as intimidating. Don't do it. In fact, don't say anything except to suggest that the client read the contract before signing it. Otherwise, you may invalidate the contract.

If you use false statements to induce someone to sign a contract, the contract can be held void as if it were never signed. Unless you carefully restate what is in the contract and can prove that your statements were accurate, an unhappy client might claim that your summary of the contract was misleading and constituted fraud.

As a professional photographer, you must find a balance between protecting yourself and scaring business away. One way to address both of these concerns is to refer to a proposed contract as an agreement. Just as photographers are uncomfortable entering into a contract to lease studio space or to buy a car, clients get nervous when asked to sign a contract. The legalese and the "small print" can be intimidating and folks are often afraid to sign something that could come back to harm them later on. Clients are often less fearful to sign an agreement than a contract (even though they are one in the same and have the same legal ramifications). You also can put your agreement in letter format, with a space at the bottom asking for the client's signature indicating that the client agrees to the terms. When potential clients refuse to sign, do not do business with them.

What to Include In a Contract

In some cases, the person who signs the contract is not the person you will be photographing. You are responsible only to the client and the client is the only one responsible to pay you. Understanding this principle can save you from having "too many bosses," each of whom wishes to direct your photography. When drafting an agreement, make sure to establish the identity of your client by having the client put her name, address, email address, phone and other contact information on the agreement.

The "four corners of a contract" axiom advises that everything that matters to you should be included in the written document. For example, if it is important that you get paid one month before the wedding, put that in the agreement. A court when enforcing the contract will not consider negotiations or agreements that are not specifically included in the contract. Don't modify an agreement anywhere other than on the agreement itself. If you think of other items that should be part of the deal after the contract is written, modify the contract.

Include in your agreement what amount and when the client will be paying, what the client gets for that payment, and when they will get it. Determine every crucial step needed to accomplish the job and specifically identify who will do what and when and where they will do it. The more precise you are, the less likely it is that problems will arise later and the more likely it is that both parties will be satisfied.

Another item to include in an agreement is a disclaimer. A disclaimer keeps you from being obligated when you or someone else screws up, as long as the screw-up was despite your best efforts. For example, if the printer loses the negatives, if your office burns down with the only copy of the photo files, or if you have a horrible accident before you get to the event, the disclaimer will protect you from having to pay damages to the client. Here's a sample disclaimer:

> The "Smith Studio" [hereinafter the "Studio"] takes the utmost care with respect to the exposure, development, and delivery of photographs. In the event the Studio fails to comply with the terms of this contract due to any event or act outside the control of the Studio, the Studio's liability is limited to the refund of fees paid.

You also may want to add a provision to your contracts that allows you to substitute another photographer in case of scheduling conflicts or illness.

If you have lots of items and restrictions in your contracts, you may get more protection, but you might very well scare away some of your customers. Use common sense and try to come up with a contract that is both balanced and fair.

                                      Photographer's Legal Guide

If you want to make a separate document part of the agreement, state specifically in the contract that the document is part of the contract and physically attach it to the contract. For example, you can attach to the contract a list of photos to be taken as part of the assignment. In the contract, state, "the photos to be taken by the photographer are listed in Attachment A." Make sure the list has the words "Attachment A" noted on it.

You may not, of course, unilaterally amend or make changes to a contract without the other's party's consent, but it's easy to modify a contract if the parties agree. Strike through the parts you are changing, add what you need, and then have all parties initial and date the changes. Just as with the original contract, be very specific when you are making changes to a contract.

Battle of the Forms—Having the Last Word

Many photographers send clients their contracts or invoices when selling their services. When the contract's terms and conditions do not fit the client's needs, you may negotiate, going back and forth via email, to reach a compromise. Sometimes clients send their contracts to the photographers in response. In this battle of the forms, which one wins? The one that stands last.

For example, you may send a client your invoice that states that payment must be paid within 30 days of delivery of the photos to the client. Your client, however, sends you a form that states that it will pay within 60 days of publication. If you take no action after receiving your client's document but go on to deliver the images, you probably will be held to the client's terms. Likewise, if your form does not mention an issue such as electronic use, but the client's form allows that use, you again will be held to the client's provisions.

To address these situations, make sure that you have the last word. You can either reply with a letter that specifically rejects the client's additional or contradictory terms or you can simply cross out each provision of concern on your client's form, put your initials and date next to each term that you have struck on the form, and return the marked-up form to your client. If the client accepts your work without responding to you, then the revised form is the binding agreement.

When dealing with clients, having the last word is important!

Retainers, Deposits, and Liquidated Damages

Photographers often ask for a nonrefundable payment to hold a date for a client's future job. If the client's plans change, the photographer will be compensated for the loss of business. What should you call that payment when dealing with a client—a retainer or deposit?

The California Supreme Court examined the word "retainer" in *Baranowski v. State Bar*, 24 Cal.3d 153 (1979). The Court explained that a "true retainer" is paid only to ensure a person's availability and does not represent payment for the performance of any services. True retainers are nonrefundable and earned when paid. But a retainer that merely represents an advance payment or security deposit for actual services to be performed in the future is not a true retainer. That payment is refundable unless fully earned.

A bride may be willing to pay for a photographer's promise to hold a certain date for her wedding, but that is probably rare. The more likely use of an advance payment to a photographer is to secure future services or products. According to the court, that makes the payment refundable unless earned.

If the client backs out of an agreement, you may be damaged because you've made travel plans or have turned down other jobs. Money can compensate you for that damage. Agreeing ahead of time on an appropriate amount of compensation is known as liquidated damages. In essence, you are fixing the amount to be paid in lieu of performance of the contract. As long as the liquidated damages are reasonable, they are enforceable.

To make sure that the liquidated damages will be paid, you simply need to make the security deposit equal to or more than the amount of those damages. You then have your liquidated damages in hand if the deal falls through. If there is any excess, you can return it to the client.

Using the words "retainer" and "deposit" in your contract may not convey what you mean. Either is appropriate to use if the amount given in advance will be fully refundable. If you want to keep the money paid up front to compensate you for loss of business if the client cancels the job, be sure to include a provision like this in your contract:

> If Client fails to perform, liquidated damages shall be charged in
> the reasonable amount of $_____.

Whatever you do, be clear and up front about your charges and your services. Your clients will be satisfied and your business will grow.

Defend, Hold Harmless and Indemnify

Photographers often are asked to sign contracts that include defend, hold harmless and indemnification clauses. Should you agree to them? It depends.

Contract language related to these defend, hold harmless and indemnification agreements typically is something like this: Photographer shall defend, indemnify, and hold harmless The Company from and against any action, suit, claim, damages, liability, costs and expenses (including reasonable attorneys' fees), arising out of or related to the use of the photo by The Company.

Your agreement to "defend" a company means that you must pay for its legal representation against claims and lawsuits. This can include the payment of expensive attorneys' fees and high litigation costs. Many companies will want to choose their legal counsel; you will have to pay for those fees as long as they are reasonable.

When you agree to "indemnify" a company, you must pay for any financial loss it incurs, such as a settlement or a court award, either directly or through reimbursement. "To hold harmless" means that you will not make a claim against a company if claims are made against you for events related to the agreement.

Agreeing to such contract provisions can be costly in the long run. In reality, however, a company rarely will seek defense costs or indemnification from the photographer unless he has done something wrong and has significant assets worth seizing. Nevertheless, you should accept these types of risks only when you understand them completely and are willing to accept the consequences.

Issues to Consider for Specific Contracts

Weddings

Since weddings are full of emotion and are expensive photographic events, a contract that specifically identifies the responsibilities of each party—you as the photographer and whoever is paying for the event—can be a life saver. The bride may not remember what you discussed during the negotiations, so written documentation can be helpful in settling disputes. Be sure to include in the contract exactly when and how you will be paid, how many hours you will be working at the wedding, the arrival time for the wedding party, and how the negatives/digital files will be handled for safekeeping after the wedding.

If the bride and groom are minors, neither can legally enter into a contract with you. Instead, a parent, guardian or friend who undertakes the responsibility to pay you must sign the contract. That person is your client. You have no recourse against the bride or groom for non-payment.

Include a model release as part of your wedding agreements so that you can be free to sell the images to other markets. If the bride and groom are minors, then you must have a parent or guardian sign the release. You will need releases from the other wedding attendees to be able to use those images commercially; the bride and groom do not have the authority to give a release on behalf of the wedding party and the guests.

Portrait Sessions

Since portraits can often be used for commercial purposes, include a model release in the contract. If you give your client copies of your digital images, restrict your client's usage of the photos to personal use. They should not have the ability to sell the prints for commercial purposes. Specify the rights you are giving your clients regarding reprints.

Establish and advise clients of your cancellation fee or require a significant non-refundable deposit. Children often get sick and can't make the scheduled session or adults may change their mind.

Book Publishing

Due to the strong bargaining position of the book publisher, book publishing contracts are usually heavily weighted in the publisher's favor. Publishers often take a large percentage of the profits after expenses are recovered and will often not allow you to sell your own books.

Get a lawyer to review book contracts on your behalf. Unless you are a highly sought-after author or have a unique book topic, you may be stuck with most or all of the standard contract terms. If you are able to firmly reject a few of them, such as the ability to purchase copies at wholesale to sell yourself or the amount of your advance you may be able to strike a more fair deal.

Liability, Model, and Property Releases

When people get hurt or incur damages, they often want to blame others. They may make a claim of liability against those they believe are responsible and those they feel are obligated to make them whole. Sometimes, those claims are misdirected, but defending those claims can take time and be costly.

A release is an agreement that shows intent to discharge another party from an existing responsibility. Since a photographer can be subject to liability claims, having a signed release in place may thwart many of them. Photographers can use releases to get permission from models to sell photos of them, to demonstrate that the photographer has permission to photograph on private property, to avoid responsibility for the inadvertent loss of the client's work, and to provide protection if the client gets hurt on the photographer's property.

Many states have adopted Uniform Commercial Code Section 1-107 which provides that a written, signed, and delivered release effectively discharges responsibility even when the release is not supported by consideration. That means that, unlike a contract, you do not have to pay or give other consideration to the person signing the release for it to be effective. Check with your attorney to determine whether UCC Section 1-107 has been enacted in your state.

A liability release discharges the photographer from responsibility for negligence that results in injury to a client when they are on the photographer's property. It also discharges responsibility for loss resulting from your actions, such as deleting the client's photos. No release will discharge you from liability for gross negligence (like being intoxicated during a photo shoot or having a hidden defect on your property that causes a client to be injured). And you will not, of course, be discharged from responsibility if you commit an intentional act such as deliberately hurting your client. It is best, however, to always have a client sign a liability

                               Photographer's Legal Guide

release because he may not realize that he can still sue you even in the case of non-dischargeable liabilities.

Model and property releases are specifically discussed in the chapter on "Restrictions on Photography."

Liability Releases – Worth the Paper They're Written On?

Many photographers who run workshops or invite customers onto their property ask their clients to sign liability releases. The releases purport to relieve photographers from a legal duty to the clients. Do they work? In some cases.

The law does not like exculpatory agreements because they encourage a lack of care, but courts recognize them in certain situations. To be effective, a release must state that the client's decision to sign the agreement was voluntary and with full knowledge of its legal consequences, among other things. Regardless of what it says, however, the agreement can release the photographer only from liability when it was caused by "ordinary negligence," not by "gross negligence" – where the photographer showed reckless or willful disregard for the client.

Many releases claim to discharge the photographer from liability for damages that the client and the client's heirs may incur. But a release can bind only the person who signs it. As a result, some courts have found that a liability release does not extinguish a client's heirs' claims for wrongful death.

What should you do to protect yourself? Get a lawyer to draft your release, have your clients sign it, operate your business as safely as you can, and get insurance just in case it's needed.

Delivery Memo

A delivery memo is the cover letter you include when sending or giving images to someone. It should include the list of images you are sending and the terms of use for those images.

Include a realistic stated value for each submitted image. While this may not be enforceable, it may be helpful to include it. You should specify the expected return date for the images, and note how the return is to be handled. You can add a "holding fee" that penalizes the person for keeping your images longer than agreed, but this also is difficult to enforce. Instead, the holding fee primarily is used to stress the importance of returning the images promptly. It is not a contract because the receiving party has not specifically agreed to do something. However, a delivery memo is a good tool to use to protect yourself because it documents what you have sent and why.

If your delivery memo's requirements are too strict, you may anger the client and lose their business. Some companies will not accept your work if you require them to sign a delivery memo or include it with your package. Review the company's submission guidelines before sending anything.

When goods are sent that have not been solicited or ordered, the recipient can consider those goods to be a gift and can keep them. Do not send prints to a publisher without the publisher's permission or request. Confirm that your original slides or negatives will be accepted, or the recipient may be legally entitled to either keep them or discard them.

Arbitration Agreements

Many contracts now include an arbitration agreement stipulating that if a dispute arises from the contract, it must be resolved by an arbitration panel or judge. People disagree about whether these are beneficial or detrimental. If you are the complaining party, the up-front costs for arbitrations can be higher than if you litigated your claim in the court system. However, the overall legal costs can be lower because arbitration allows only for minimal pre-trial discovery and because the arbitration process is relatively quick. By comparison, it can take years for a case to go through the court system. When you may be subject to liability, you can limit your exposure a bit better with an arbitration clause in your release or contract. The damages often are limited and can be more reasonable, especially when compared to a runaway jury verdict.

Before agreeing to a contract that includes an arbitration agreement clause, be sure that you have input as to the choice of the arbitrator. Whether the American Arbitration Association or another group that you trust conducts the arbitration, it generally is best that the arbitration be conducted according to the American Arbitration Association rules. You also want to demand that the arbitration take place in a convenient location.

Lease Agreements

Photographers often need to rent studio or office space. It's best to have an attorney review any lease agreement before you sign it. Standard leases often are biased in the favor of the landlord and an attorney will know which terms may be negotiated more fairly. A lease agreement should specify the length of the lease, the penalties for breaking the lease, the monthly lease payment. It should note whether improvements can be made to the property, and which activities—if any—are prohibited on the property. Do not assume that a lease agreement cannot be modified. Everything is negotiable, especially when the landlord's property has been vacant for a while.

Warranties in Sales Contracts

Warranties provide certain guarantees related to a product or to a service. You may voluntarily include a warranty that guarantees either the quality of your product and/or your future contract-related performance. Here is an example of a warranty:

Your investment in this photograph is protected. This print comes with a lifetime warranty and will be replaced free of charge if lost, stolen, or damaged.

This is known as an express warranty because you have specifically and voluntarily stated it. It helps to bring in business and build customer confidence and satis-faction.

Implied warranties are sometimes made part of a contract, too, by state law rather than by expressly including them in the contract. If you are a merchant providing goods that have been contracted for, there is—unless specifically disclaimed—an implied warranty. The implied warranty requires that the goods are such that they would "pass in the trade under the contract description" and are "fit for the ordinary purposes for which such goods are used." In other words, when you sell prints or photos, they should be of the quality and condition that would normally be expected. If you, as the seller, have reason to know that the buyer wants the goods for a particular purpose and the buyer is relying on your skill and judgment in selecting/preparing those goods, then there is an implied warranty of fitness for the particular purpose unless it also is specifically disclaimed.

Some implied warranties can be renounced. Except for free and clear title of the goods, implied warranties are disclaimed by using language such as "as is" and "prints may fade in time." You also may disclaim implied warranties specifically by stating that the "warranties of merchantability and fitness are excluded."

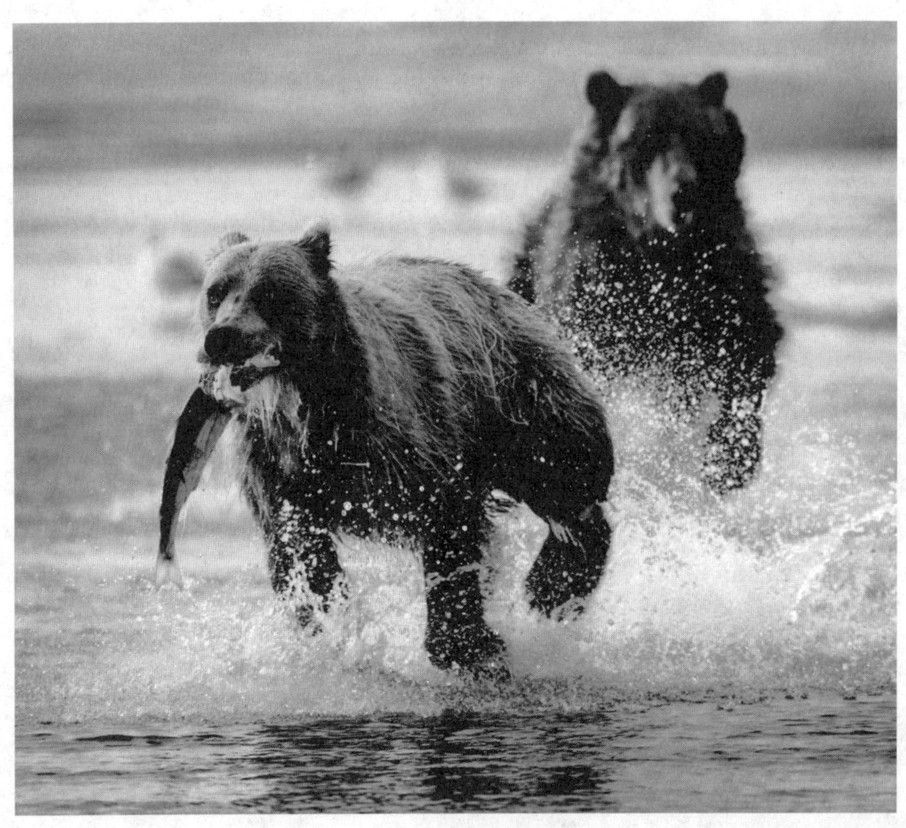

Copyright 2006 Carolyn E. Wright

RESTRICTIONS ON PHOTOGRAPHY

Restrictions on Photographing People - Rights of Privacy

In general, when people are in public, you may photograph them. The use of the photographs can be restricted due to certain privacy rights. The rights of a person to certain kinds of privacy are recognized in most states, but the specific laws are different for each one. It is, therefore, tricky to know what you can do. The safest approach is to follow the most restrictive regulations.

Privacy rights can be subdivided into four areas. The first is "invasion of privacy" or "intrusion upon another's seclusion." This happens when someone actually enters a person's private domain in a manner that would be considered offensive to the average person. As a photographer, the act of going on someone's land without permission would be trespassing and may violate their right of privacy. You don't have to take a photo or publish an image photo for the action to be unlawful. Some courts have found that a photographer has violated privacy rights even when photographing someone in public. Instances would include cases where the photographers harass their subjects, use hidden cameras, or wait for a woman's skirt to be blown at a fun house. It also is unlawful to view and photograph people inside of residences or other places where privacy is normally expected, even when the photographer is standing in public.

The second right of privacy is violated when private facts are publicly disclosed. This law is difficult to enforce; if the disclosed information is true, courts usually find that First Amendment (freedom of speech and the press) interests outweigh privacy rights. Violation of these privacy rights when an ordinary person would consider the information private and the disclosure offensive. Because of the required elements, photographers rarely run into trouble here.

The third right of privacy requires that you not portray a person in false light. This right is often violated when photographs are published, usually because of the caption. For a violation to occur, it requires that someone be publicly portrayed in a false manner that an ordinary person would find offensive. To be liable, the publisher of the photograph must have known of or recklessly disregarded the probable falsity of what is represented. A violation here is similar to defamation when someone's reputation is damaged by a statement that is known or should be known to be false. False light does not require that the person was damaged.

The fourth right of privacy is an important concern for photographers. It involves the commercial appropriation of someone's name or likeness. This is also known as the right of publicity. Violations occur when someone uses the names or likenesses of others without their consent to gain some benefit. They usually occur when photographs of people are used in advertisements or trade (when the photos are incorporated into a product, such as on coffee mugs) without their permission. That is why model releases are so important; they document that you have people's permission to use their photograph for certain or for any purposes.

Commercial vs. Editorial Use of Photographs of People

When photographers take photos of people, they must be careful to not invade their privacy. After the photo is taken, however, the photographer should be concerned with the person's right of publicity. You violate a person's right of publicity when, without permission, you use a photo of a person for your own benefit. The editorial use of a photo is not considered a use of the person's image for your own benefit. Commercial use is different. Commercial use clearly benefits the photographer, so you need the person's consent to use their image. If you get a model release signed by the subject, you are free to use the image commercially, i.e., for advertising. But what exactly is the difference between editorial use and commercial use?

If an image is used in a newsworthy item then that constitutes an editorial use. In such cases, a person's rights are evaluated in light of constitutional interests. "Newsworthiness" is a First Amendment, freedom of the press interest and is broadly construed. Courts traditionally have defined public interest or newsworthiness in liberal and far-reaching terms, not limiting it to the dissemination of news in the sense of current events. They have extended it well beyond that to include all types of factual, educational and historical data, even including entertainment and amusement and other interesting phases of human activity in general.

Commercial use of a photograph usually occurs when the picture of the person has been used purely for "advertising purposes." While the photograph of a person may be used for something that is sold for profit, such as for use in a book or as a photographic print, selling the photo is not the test for a commercial usage.

Using a picture of a person in advertising or for trade without consent may violate the person's right of publicity, especially when it injures the economic interests of the person due to commercial exploitation. If someone looking at a photograph would think that the person in it is promoting or endorsing a product affiliated with the photograph, then the use is commercial. When the photo of a person is incorporated into a product such as a tee shirt, the use is commercial. At times, it is difficult to determine if a usage is considered commercial or editorial, so it is always safer to get the model release.

Even when a photo is used editorially, the person in the photo can get upset. Take, for example, an incident involving Britney Spears and her then husband, Kevin Federline. They were promised complete privacy during their October honeymoon in the Fiji islands. No members of the paparazzi were there to intrude. But the couple allowed the resort's staff members to photograph them enjoying their honeymoon when assured that the photos were for personal use and would be placed in a souvenir album to be given to the couple. One staff

member, however, sold the photos to US Weekly Magazine, and a full spread
was published. Britney was furious. She hadn't signed a model release. Did the
photographer violate her rights of privacy? Not likely.

Britney can allege that the photographer "invaded her privacy" or "intruded upon
her seclusion." This happens when someone actually intrudes a person's private
domain in a manner that would be considered offensive to the average person.
She had, however, agreed to have her photo taken, so a court probably would find
that the use of the photo in a manner other than she expected did not affect her
rights. Britney also might have claimed that her right of publicity—the commercial appropriation of her name or likeness—was violated. This, however, would
likely be unsuccessful since her honeymoon was a "newsworthy" item (and First
Amendment concerns would surely have overridden her protests).

In a statement to The Associated Press, US Weekly said: "Coming from a celebrity who sold pictures of both her wedding and her stepdaughter, it's unlikely the
issue here is privacy. Could it be that Britney is seeing red after not seeing the
green from these photos? Britney Spears should start a magazine if she'd like to
dictate her own coverage."

Editorial Use of Person's Photograph Is Confirmed

Fortunately for photographers, the law on editorial use recently was confirmed.
From 1999 until 2001, a photographer named Philip-Lorca diCorcia took photos
of people in Times Square. His camera was set on a tripod and strobe lights were
placed across the street. The project culminated in an exhibition called "Heads" at
the Pace/MacGill Gallery in Chelsea, New York.

One of shots from the project was of Erno Nussenzweig, an Orthodox Jew and
retired diamond merchant from Union City, N.J. He sued diCorcia and Pace
for exhibiting and publishing the portrait without his permission and for profit-
ing from it. He asked the court for an injunction to stop sales and publication of
the photograph, for $500,000 in compensatory damages, and for $1.5 million in
punitive damages. Of note, Nussenzweig complained that use of the photograph
violated his constitutional right to practice his religion, which prohibits the use of
graven images.

In an affidavit submitted to the court on Mr. diCorcia's behalf, Peter Galassi,
Chief Curator of Photography at the Museum of Modern Art, said, "If the
law were to forbid artists to exhibit and sell photographs made in public places
without the consent of all who might appear in those photographs, then artistic
expression in the field of photography would suffer drastically. If such a ban were
projected retroactively, it would rob the public of one of the most valuable tradi-
tions of our cultural inheritance."

The judge in the case dismissed the suit on First Amendment grounds stating
that such photographs are the price every person must pay for a society where information and opinion freely flows. While Nussenzweig has appealed the judg-

ment, the good news is that photographers may continue to photograph people in public and may use those shots editorially without the person's permission.

Editorial Use—Book Cover

Many photographers assume that since a book cover helps to sell a book, a photo placed there must be a commercial use. That assumption recently was proven wrong.

Thais Cardoso Almeida's photograph was published on the cover of a book called "Anjos Proibidos" or "Forbidden Angels." Amazon.com posted the book cover on its website as part of a sales listing. Almeida sued Amazon in Florida basing her case on right of publicity, civil theft, and invasion of privacy claims. The Florida court awarded summary judgment to Amazon on all claims and Almeida appealed to the 11th Circuit Court of Appeals.

The 11th Circuit affirmed summary judgment for Amazon. In sum, it held that Amazon's incidental display of photographs from the cover or inside of a book was not for a commercial purpose. Amazon's display of the book cover (that includes Almeida's photograph) was no different than the experience provided by a bookstore when it displays a book for its customers. The court ruled against a right of publicity claim.

Model Release

It is a good idea to get model releases from anyone you photograph, not just from professional models. They are used to document that: (1) the person you are photographing has given you permission to photograph him; and (2) you may use the photograph for listed purposes. The release should state these two items specifically. Use as broad of language for the possible uses of the photo as you can. You do not need to include extraneous, unnecessary language stating that the model has capacity to contract or that the photographer retains the copyright. These are implied provisions determined by laws outside of the contract. Including extra information and making the release longer than needed might frighten the model or subject.

You should use different model releases to address your specific needs. The general model release can be as simple as:

> I give Carolyn Wright or her assigns permission to use and
> publish photos in which I appear without incurring any debts or
> liabilities of any kind.
>
> Name (print) ____________________________________
> Address ____________________________________
> City/State/Zip________________________________
> Signature __________________________________
> Parent/guardian's signature __________________

and as complex as a multi-page document. The simple release may not cover all uses of the photo. Given the current use of technology, you also may want to include a provision that allows for digital manipulation of the photo. The American Society of Media Photographers offers a release module for free at www.asmp. org/releases. If you're an ASMP member, you get access to a customizable release module that allows you to modify the release for your needs and print the final version from your Internet browser. Contact an attorney for assistance with your more complicated circumstances.

Consideration (payment in some form) for signing the release is not needed in many states. For additional information, see the Contracts chapter on releases.

General Release

While some famous people come to hate the paparazzi, they certainly seem to like to have their picture taken early in their career. At that time, photographers often can get a "general" model release for those photographs (without any restrictions as to the use of the images) easily and for no or little charge. Will that general model release be valid years later when the star is making millions or if the photographer makes a lot of money from the pictures? The likely answer is yes.

In the recent case of Marder v. Lopez, the Ninth Circuit Court of Appeals affirmed the validity of a general release relating to the movie "Flashdance." The movie was purportedly based on Maureen Marder's life. Marder sued Jennifer Lopez, Sony Music, and Paramount Pictures for using "well-known scenes from Flashdance" in one of Lopez's music videos. Marder made claims of copyright infringement and violation of her rights of publicity (among others).

Marder had signed a general release in 1982 giving Paramount the right to use her life story. The Court found that, "though in hindsight the agreement appears to be unfair to Marder—she only received $2300 in exchange for release of all claims relating to a movie that grossed over $150 million—there is simply no evidence that her consent was obtained by fraud, deception, misrepresentation, duress, or undue influence."

Similarly, Russian tennis player, Anastasia Myskina, who then was 20 years old, posed for photographs by Mark Seliger. Seliger first photographed Myskina for the Gentleman's Quarterly's 2002 "Sports" issue and then photographed her topless. Myskina had signed a model release that said she consented to the use of her name and the pictures by the magazine and by "others it may authorize, for editorial purposes."

After winning the French Open in 2004, a Russian newspaper published the topless photos. Myskina filed an $8 million lawsuit against the publisher, Conde Nast Publications Inc., Gentleman's Quarterly, and Seliger alleging emotional distress and economic injury.

The New York judge who presided over the case held that Myskina's rights were not violated despite her insistence that she did not understand the release and was not fluent in English at the time. Instead, the Judge stated that, "absent allegations of fraud, duress or some other wrongdoing, Myskina's claimed misunderstanding of the release's terms does not excuse her from being bound on the contract. Nor can she avoid her obligations under the release because of her purported failure to read its contents."

Even though the photographer allegedly told Myskina that the topless photos were for "himself," the Judge found that the oral agreement contradicted the plain language of the written agreement and was not admissible. The Judge then dismissed the case.

Try to get a general model release from anyone you photograph, even when you don't expect that you'll need it later.

Dealing With Models and Model Releases

Several unique issues can arise when dealing with models and model releases. You must take steps to defend a challenge from the model that he did not or could not legally sign the release.

Model's Identity

When you ask a person to sign a model release, also try to get a copy of his driver's license, birth certificate, or passport to attach to the release. This helps you if the model later claims he did not sign the release. It also proves that the model had the legal capacity (not being a minor) to enter a contract. It gives you additional protection if you are shooting nudes. The model should be at least the age of majority (in most states, it is 18). The best practice is not to take a nude or partially-nude photograph of anyone—including babies—under the age of majority so that you can avoid any allegations of child pornography.

Model Vouchers

When you ask a professional model to sign a model release, ask first if she has signed a "model voucher." When you hire a model from a modeling agency, she often has signed a voucher that gives the agency the rights to the images. Even if you have the model sign a general release, it will not be valid because the earlier specific model voucher supercedes yours. If a model does not know whether he has signed a model voucher, then you can ask him to sign a "model voucher disclosure form," which gives you protection if you distribute images beyond the scope of the model voucher.

Models in Foreign Countries

When you travel to foreign countries to photograph the people there, do you need a model release? What if the people don't speak English?

                        Photographer's Legal Guide

Nevada Wier has published thousands of travel photographs from all over the world. In her book, Adventure Travel Photography, she advises:

> If you plan to use your photographs for publication or stock, I think it is wise to have signed model releases from any people you photograph in a foreign city, no matter what their nationality or what the shooting situation is. . . . Translate your release forms into the language of the country you'll be traveling and photographing in. In more remote regions it is a bit trickier to get signed model releases, and not always appropriate. People may be suspicious, confused or frightened if they're asked to sign a piece of paper. Use your common sense.

As a photographer, it is important to protect yourself as much as possible. Fortunately, the model release is one way that has been proven to be effective. Be sure to consider rights of privacy issues before you click the shutter or use an image.

Restrictions on Photographing Property

In general, if property is visible and can be photographed from a public place, you don't need a property release to use an image that depicts the property and you may use the photo in any manner. Copyright law provides an exclusion for photographing buildings located on property, but not for statues or other items that may have separate copyrights. There also are restrictions on some governmental property. These include federal seals and insignia as well as military or nuclear installations due to security concerns. If the statue or copyrighted item has minimal presence in your image, your photo may fall under the exclusion due to fair use. Otherwise, you must get permission to take an image and to use it for any purpose.

Nevertheless, some companies have tried to prevent the use—both commercially and editorially—of photographs of their buildings or objects via trademark protection or contract law. Examples include the Rock and Roll Hall of Fame, the Lone Cypress tree on the 17 Mile Drive at Pebble Beach, CA, and the "Hollywood" sign. While these attempts have been unsuccessful, it can be expensive to litigate them. Is it worth it to you to spend thousands of dollars to test this issue? That's a choice you'll have to make. On the other hand, photographers should protect their rights. If you know you are legally entitled to photograph a subject, exercise that right.

In sum, a model or property release may not be legally necessary when photographing certain subjects, but getting one may help. It may make some people think that they can't sue you (they can, even if their cause of action is bogus). If they do sue you, having a release may shorten the litigation and could help you win. Even when you win, though, your defense fees can be costly.

Some stock agencies may require a property or model release although it may not be legally required. It just means that they are being cautious in this litigious society.

What is often practical is not always a legal requirement. When trying to decide whether a release is required, talk to an attorney to discuss your particular needs.

Restrictions When Photographing on Federal Lands

Photographers love to create images depicting the treasures of our national parks. But if you look too much like a professional with a tripod or long lens, you might get hassled by Park Rangers who insist that you have a permit or who try to curtail your photography. Are they within their rights? It depends.

Photography in national parks falls under "Special Park Uses" and is addressed in Director's Order #53 located at http://www.nps.gov/policy/DOrders/DOrder53.html. A "special park use" is a short-term activity that takes place in a park area and:

- provides a benefit to an individual, group or organization, rather than to the public at large;

- requires written authorization and some degree of management control from the National Park Service ["NPS"] in order to protect park resources and the public interest;

- is not prohibited by law or regulation; and

- is neither initiated, sponsored, nor conducted by the NPS.

Fortunately, Section 14 of D.O. #53 specifically provides an exception to the written authorization requirement for photography. It states that a permit is not required for:

- a visitor using a camera and/or a recording device for his/her own personal use and within normal visitation areas and hours;

- a commercial photographer not using a prop, model, or set, and staying within normal visitation areas and hours; or

- press coverage of breaking news.

This fits the profile of most photographers, even pros. Be sure, however, to get a permit when your photography:

- involves the use of a model, set, or prop;

                                                    Photographer's Legal Guide

- requires entry into a closed area; or

- requires access to the park before or after normal working hours.

In addition, you will need a permit if you are bringing a group into the park for photographic instruction. Recently, the regulations have been revised to require payment of a fee if your activities require a permit.

Any activity, including photography, must not:

- cause injury or damage to park resources;

- be contrary to the purposes for which the park was established;

- unreasonably impair the atmosphere of peace and tranquility maintained in wilderness, natural, historic or commemorative locations within the park;

- unreasonably interfere with interpretive programs, visitor services, other scheduled activities, or with the administrative activities of the NPS;

- substantially impair the operation of public facilities or services of NPS concessionaires or contractors;

- present a clear and present danger to public health and safety; or

- result in significant conflict with other existing uses.

At the time of this writing, D.O. #53 lists a "sunset date" of December 2006 or "when superseded." A sunset law requires administrative bodies to periodically justify their existence to the legislature. Keep an eye open for changes.

For now, we all may photograph our beautiful national parks to our heart's content. Keep a copy of D.O. #53 in your camera bag to share with the Ranger, if needed. And if you get harassed, contact an attorney to determine your rights and remedies.

Restrictions on Flying With Your Equipment

The Transportation Security Administration's ("TSA") mission is to "protect the Nation's transportation systems to ensure freedom of movement for people and commerce." The TSA, not the airlines, determines what you can carry into the secured area of an airport.

It's great that the TSA allows photographers an extra bag of "photographic equipment" in addition to one (1) carry-on and one (1) personal item through the screening checkpoint. The additional bag must conform to your air carrier's carry-on restrictions for size and weight." The guideline can be found at: http://www.tsa.gov/public/display?content=090005198006b11c.

The catch here is that your airline has the right to disallow the third bag; many airlines have simply chosen not to agree to the TSA policy on a third bag. While you can get it through security, you may be forced to check it at the gate. If you take two carry-on bags of photography equipment plus a briefcase for your laptop, you may have to have one of the carry-ons checked if the third bag is disallowed.

E-mail messages to Delta, Northwest, Alaska, United and American Airlines asking whether they allow the extra photography bag either were not returned or the responses quoted/referred to baggage guidelines from their websites that allow only two pieces of carry-on luggage. Even if any of the replies had been positive, the rules may be applied differently at the gate.

The safest plan is to go with two carry-on bags, at least for now.

Customs Issues When Traveling Abroad

Photographers often carry a lot of expensive gear when traveling abroad. When returning to the United States, if the border agent believes that you bought the equipment while out of the country, you will have to pay customs duties on those items. These duties can be significant because of the value of the gear. The trick is to document your equipment before you leave.

Prior to your departure, prepare a "Certificate of Registration" form (CBP Form 4457) for your personal articles, including cameras and laptops. Include the serial numbers of your items on the list. The certificate is your proof of ownership and will exempt your property from customs duties. More information is available at www.cbp.gov/xp/cgov/travel/clearing_goods/certificate_of_registration.xml. The form may be printed at: www.cbp.gov/linkhandler/cgov/toolbox/forms/4457.ctt/cbp_4457.pdf.

Before you leave the country, take your equipment and the completed form to your local U.S. Customs and Border Protection ("CBP") office. You may locate an office convenient to you at www.cbp.gov/xp/cgov/toolbox/contacts/ports/. A CBP officer will compare your items with those listed on the form, sign the form, and return it to you. Keep it with you when re-entering the United States to avoid large customs duties on equipment that you owned before you left the United States. Note that any repairs performed on the equipment while out of the country are subject to customs duties. Keep the form for future trips, as well, as it is valid for the registered articles as long as the form is legible. You may laminate it for better safekeeping.

Before you take your next photography trip abroad, do some important preventive work for that dreaded customs inspection on the trip home.

Trademarks/Trademarked Items in Photographs

Photographers often take pictures that depict trademarks or trademarked items. Trademarks are words, symbols, packaging, colors, sounds, scents or a combination of these that allow people to identify the source of goods or services. (Additional information on trademarks is available in the chapter on "Getting Started With Your Business.") Infringing a trademark occurs when the use of the mark causes likelihood of confusion as to the source of the product or service. When you include a trademarked item in a photo, have you infringed the trademark? The University of Alabama apparently thinks so.

Daniel Moore is well known for painting some of the greatest moments in Alabama's football history. They usually include one of Alabama's trademarks—a script "A," Alabama's mascot (an elephant), or the words "Crimson Tide," "Bama," and "Roll Tide." Moore's prints have increased in value over the years, with some now worth $2,500. He has a strong following of Alabama fans. But he has sold his artwork for years without having a licensing agreement with the University in place. After several threats, the University sued Moore in early 2006 demanding that he pay the University royalties on all of his paintings.

Licensing of trademarks is a source of tremendous income for many businesses, especially sports teams. Further, the University has claimed that Moore's failure to pay royalties dilutes the value of their assets.

In a similar case in 1998, Tiger Woods sued Rick Rush's company for selling copies of a print of the golfer without his permission. The artist successfully claimed that First Amendment rights trumped the celebrity's ability to protect the rights to his likeness. But that case turned on an analysis of Woods' rights of privacy/publicity. For Moore, the issue is whether trademarks have been infringed.

Trademarks are infringed when there is a "likelihood of confusion" as to the source, affiliation, or sponsorship of the goods or services. The evidence often used in such cases is an extensive survey of consumers as to whether they are confused about the source of the product. According to polls taken by the University of Alabama, more than 10 percent of those asked believed that the school was sponsoring or approving some of Moore's (unlicensed) work.

"All this is hurtful to Daniel because they've made it seem as if he has made himself wealthy by traveling on the tradition of Alabama as if he is a hitchhiker who has no merit of his own," said his attorney, Stephen Heninger. "Both Daniel and the University have benefited from his work."

Moore has promised other artists that he will not settle the case if it means that his First Amendment rights are compromised. If he loses, he'll have to pay three times the amount of royalties he would have paid the University if he had licensed the prints. Interestingly, the University has not sued other artists who have produced work without the University's approval.

It will be some time before the court issues its opinion. In the meantime, be aware that when you sell photographs of trademarks or trademarked items, the trademark owner may aggressively attempt to stop you from selling your work or seek licensing fees from you.

New Law Affects Photos of Trademarks

Recent proposed amendments to trademark law raised concerns as to whether it would be more difficult for photographers to include trademarks in their photos. The good news is that the final language of the new law is more favorable than we feared.

The Trademark Dilution Revision Act ("TDRA") became effective October 6, 2006. The Act establishes a "likelihood of dilution" standard rather than "actual dilution" when a challenged and allegedly diluting mark has already been put into use. The new law also provides for relief from both dilution by blurring and dilution by tarnishment. Dilution by blurring occurs when "an association arising from the similarity between a mark or trade name and a famous mark that impairs the distinctiveness of the famous mark." Dilution by tarnishment happens when the mark is used in an unsavory or unwholesome manner or it is used in connection with an inferior trademark. A famous mark now means it is nationally famous and is "widely recognized by the general consuming public of the United States as a designation of source of the goods or services of the mark's owner."

Of specific concern to photographers were suggested revisions to the "fair use exceptions" for trademarks. The proposal eliminated "noncommercial use of a mark" and changed the fair use definition. Fortunately, the final TRDA maintained the "noncommercial use" exception. The fair use exception has been revised to include "any fair use, including a nominative or descriptive fair use, or facilitation of such fair use." This language appears to be more inclusive than that originally proposed. You still may use a trademark in all forms of news reporting and commentary.

While the final affect of the TDRA won't be known until the courts interpret it, photographers can breathe a bit easier when shooting photos that include trademarks.

 Photographer's Legal Guide

Appendix

Recommended Photography Associations

Advertising Photographers of America (APA)

http://www.apanational.com/
Advertising Photographers of America 's mission is successful advertising photographers. Its goal is to establish, endorse, and promote professional practices, standards, and ethics in the photographic and advertising community. It seeks to mentor, motivate, educate, and inspire in the pursuit of excellence. Its aim is to champion and speak as one common voice for advertising photographers and image makers to the advertising industry in the United States and the World.

American Society of Media Photographers (ASMP)

http://www.asmp.org/
The American Society of Media Photographers was established in 1944 to further the interests of photographers and their profession. It is a resource for community, culture, commerce, and publications relating to publication photography.

American Society of Picture Professionals (ASPP)

http://www.aspp.com/
The American Society of Picture Professionals is a nationwide organization of professionals who produce, sell, edit, catalog and use photographic imagery and is a forum for education, information, dialogue, interaction and professional growth. ASPP provides an open exchange of information on industry ethics and standards, business practices, and needs created by new technology.

Editorial Photographers (EP)

http://www.editorialphoto.com/
Editorial Photographers is a non-profit organization dedicated to improving the health and profitability of editorial photography. Its mission is to educate photographers and photography buyers about business issues affecting our industry and in the process raise the level of business practices in the profession.

North American Nature Photographers Association (NANPA)

http://www.nanpa.org/
North American Nature Photographers Association promotes the art and science of nature photography as a medium of communication for nature appreciation and environmental protection. NANPA provides education and inspiration, gathers and disseminates information, and develops standards for all persons interested in the field of nature photography. NANPA fosters professionalism and ethical conduct in all aspects of its endeavors.

NATIONAL PRESS PHOTOGRAPHERS ASSOCIATION (NPPA)

http://www.nppa.org/
The National Press Photographers Association is dedicated to the advancement of photojournalism, its creation, editing and distribution, in all news media. NPPA encourages photojournalists to reflect high standards of quality in their professional performance and in their personal code of ethics. NPPA vigorously promotes freedom of the press in all its forms. To this end, NPPA provides continuing educational programs and fraternalism without bias, as it supports and acknowledges the best the profession has to offer.

PICTURE ARCHIVE COUNCIL OF AMERICA (PACA)

http://www.pacaoffice.org/
The Picture Archive Council of America's mission is to foster and protect the interests of the picture archive community through advocacy, education and communication. Its purposes are to develop useful business standards, to promote ethical business practices, to actively advocate copyright protection and copyright education, to collect and disseminate accurate information relevant to the members, their contributing artists and clients, to take an active role in the developments affecting the picture archive community, and to build and maintain relationships with other professional organizations and related industries.

PICTURE LICENSING UNIVERSAL SYSTEM (PLUS)

http://www.useplus.com/
Picture Licensing Universal System is an international non-profit trade association with a tightly focused mission: "To simplify and facilitate the licensing of images." In the PLUS Coalition, photographers, illustrators, stock picture agencies, artist representatives, advertising agencies, advertisers, graphic design firms, publishers, and associated industries and initiatives have joined forces to create a universal licensing language.

PROFESSIONAL PHOTOGRAPHERS OF AMERICA (PPA)

http://www.ppa.com
Professional Photographers of America is the world's largest not-for-profit association for professional photographers, with more than 17,000 members in 64 countries. It seeks to increase its members' business savvy as well as broaden their creative scope. It aims to advance their careers by providing them with all the tools for success.

STOCK ARTISTS ALLIANCE (SAA)

http://www.stockartistsalliance.org/Index.htm
Founded in 2001, the Stock Artists Alliance is an international organization of photographers who produce images for rights—protected license. The mission of the SAA is to protect and promote the business interests of its members with regard to the worldwide distribution of their intellectual property.

Wedding & Portrait Photographers International (WPPI)

http://www.wppionline.com/
Wedding Photographers International has grown to be the largest trade show and convention in professional photography. The association works to meet the needs of wedding, portrait, commercial, photojournalism and fine art photographers. WPPI, together with Rangefinder Magazine, is dedicated to the education of professional photographers and the continued elevation of imaging.

Women in Photography International (WIPI)

http://www.womeninphotography.org/
Founded in 1981, Women In Photography International is a 501.c.3 outreach organization that promotes the visibility of women photographers and their work.

Recommended Reading

Business and Legal Forms for Photographers by Tad Crawford, Esq.

Crawford's book provides form contracts for photographers. It includes a CD of the forms so that you can easily revise them to fit your individual needs. It also explains the purpose of each proposed contract clause.

Legal Handbook for Photographers by Bert P. Krages, Esq.

Krages' book explains the legal principles that affect photographer's rights to make images. It provides guidance on how to handle confrontations, how to obtain remedies if wronged, and how to develop an ethic that reflects your individual approach to photography.

Licensing Photography by Richard Weisgrau and Victor S. Perlman, Esq.

Co-written by a professional photographer and an intellectual property attorney, this book is a comprehensive guide to licensing your photographs.

Self–Employed Tax Solutions by June Walker

Walker's book is an easy–to–read and understand guide to money saving and audit–proof tax and recordkeeping for independent professionals.

Small Business Taxes Made Easy by Eva Rosenberg

Written by an Enrolled Agent licensed by the IRS and known as "TaxMama," Rosenberg's book covers tips and guidelines to cut your tax bill and gain the greatest possible advantage out of each IRS rule and regulation.

Recommended Websites

- **http://www.photoattorney.com**—weekly blog on the law for photographers and updates to the *Photographer's Legal Guide*

- **http://www.copyright.gov**—U.S. Copyright Office website

- **http://www.uspto.gov**—U.S. Patent and Trademark Office website

- **http://williampatry.blogspot.com**—in depth legal analysis of copyright law

- **http://www.pdnonline.com**—Photo District News website, including news on copyright, court cases, business issues, legal, and legislative matters.

- **http://www.taxmama.com**—tax information and updates from an Enrolled Agent licensed by the IRS and the U.S. Treasury Department

Yahoo® Groups—Free Online Email Communities

APAnet is a professional discussion group open to topics directly related to the business of advertising photography, sponsored by Advertising Photographers of America. Participation is open to both APA members and non-members alike.

The **Controlled Vocabulary group** is for people who wish to engage in discussions related to the use of Controlled Vocabularies, Hierarchies, Thesauri, and Classification schemes used in databases, with a specific interest in image databases. Other topics of interest, such as the use of IPTC meta data, Dublin Core, XML, and Adobe Photoshop's XMP data format are fair game as well. For additional details see the parent website: http://www.ControlledVocabulary.com/

The **Stockphoto Network** mailing list has been set up to serve as an extensive resource for professional stock photographers, photographic libraries, stock photography buyers, and anyone else interested in the stock photography industry.

ASMPproAdvice is a place where students and emerging photographers can discuss issues and seek answers to questions related to commercial photography from established, experienced working professionals. This is not a forum for amateur photo concerns. This list is open to both ASMP members and non-members.

Various Website Resources

Pricing Resources

http://photographersindex.com/stockprice.htm
http://www.fotoquote.com

Electronic Image Tracking

http://www.picscout.com
https://www.digimarc.com/mypicturemarc
http://www.ideeinc.com

Business Software

http://www.fotobiz.net
http://quickbooks.com
http://www.zimberoff.com/photobyte.htm
http://turbotax.inuit.com

Quick Tips

10 Quick Tips To Protect Your Images from Infringement

1. Use the copyright "notice"—the © with a date and name of the copyright owner—whenever you publish your images. It may stop someone from copying an image, either because the person will be reminded that the image belongs to someone or because the notice impairs the image for the person's use.

2. Include with your copyright notice the words "All Rights Reserved." Some additional international protection is added.

3. Register your copyrights with the US Copyright Office. While you own the copyright to your image when you click the shutter (in most instances), registration itself provides some evidence that the image is yours. Register it even if it's already published. It's better late than never.

4. If you find a website that is unlawfully using one of your images, follow the provisions of the Digital Millennium Copyright Act to contact the Internet Service Provider who must then remove the material from user's website.

5. When you provide copies of your images to someone else, put in writing the specific rights of usage you are giving that person.

6. Put a copyright notice on your website, such as: All photographs appearing on this site are the property of Carolyn Wright Photography. They are protected by the US copyright laws, and are not to be downloaded or reproduced in any way without the written permission of Carolyn Wright Photography.

7. Don't steal others work, such as music. Get a license if you need a tune to accompany your slideshow. Teach your children and others to respect other's work.

8. Read the fine print whenever you submit your image to anyone/anywhere to make sure that it's not a license agreement to use your image or to transfer the copyright.

9. Include your copyrights in your estate planning, along with your other assets such as your house and furnishings.

10. Sue those who steal your work. Send the message that you value your work.

10 Quick Tips for Model Releases

1. You don't need a model release if the photo is used editorially, which includes news items, textbooks, and public interest items. You definitely need it for advertising and trade uses. Since uses can fall between those two extremes, it's safer to have a release than not.

2. Draft the release to be as broad as possible so that you can use the photo for any future need that arises without having to go back to the model.

3. Photograph the model signing the release and/or make a photograph of his driver's license to file with the release as proof that the model himself signed it.

4. If you are photographing a minor (usually under 18), have the parent or the legal guardian sign the release. Get both parents' signatures if you can.

5. Get the release before the shoot so you don't waste your time photographing the model if she is not going to agree to sign it.

6. File copies of the releases off site in case the originals are destroyed.

7. While many states do not require consideration/payment for the release, some do. If you include consideration, make sure that it is fair so that a court won't find your release invalid.

8. If the person is not identifiable in the photograph, you don't need a release. Sometimes, however, a person can be recognized even when you can't see his face.

9. Just because a person consents to have her photo taken does not give you the right to use the image in any way you want.

10. Get the model release in writing, even from friends and family.

10 Quick Tips for Photographer's Rights

1. In general, if you are in a place with public access, you may take photographs of whatever you want. What you do with those photos depends on a variety of issues.

2. Property owners may restrict your activities, including photography, while on the owners' property, but owners may not keep you from photographing property from another place.

3. Photography can be restricted by commanders of military installations for national security interests and by the Department of Energy for nuclear facilities.

4. You may photograph anyone in a public area except when the person has an expectation of privacy (such as in a restroom, a hospital, or a dressing room).

5. You may not block public access areas or create hazardous conditions with your activities, including photography.

6. Anyone, including security guards and police officers, may ask questions about your photography activities, but you do not have to respond. Some states require that you identify yourself to police officers.

7. Harassment and coercion by anyone are illegal.

8. No one, except law enforcement, may detain you unless you commit a crime in that person's presence.

9. Persons other than law enforcement personnel do not have the right to confiscate your film/digital card. Police officers may take your film/cards when making an arrest or when they have a warrant.

10. If your rights as a photographer are violated, contact an attorney to understand your options.

About the Author

Carolyn E. Wright is an attorney whose practice is aimed squarely at the needs of photographers. Carolyn understands the special issues that confront both professional and amateur photographers alike.

A professional photographer herself, Carolyn has the credentials and the experience to protect your rights. Carolyn has practiced law with Atlanta law firms, including King & Spalding (one of the top 50 firms in the nation), for more than a decade. She has represented Fortune 100 clients in multimillion dollar litigation, but wants to help photographers with their careers. Carolyn provides legal information for photographers for free on her weekly blog: www.photoattorney.com.

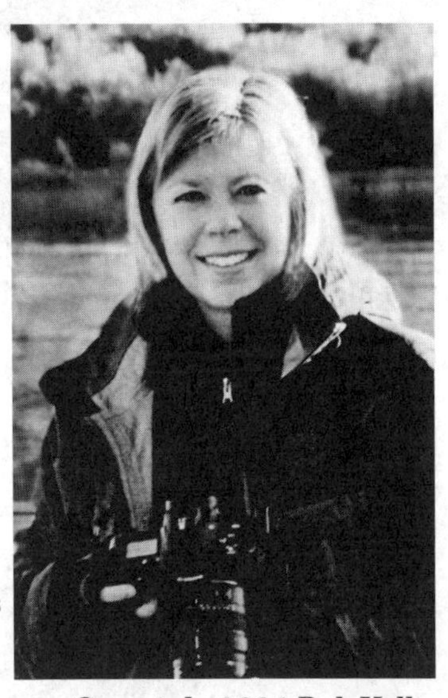
Copyright 2006 Bob Keller

While her legal credentials are among the best in the business, Carolyn thinks it is important to keep ties with the photographic community. That's why she maintains an active photography business. Her photos are included in the photo book, *"Captivating Wildlife—Images from the Top 10 Emerging Wildlife Photographers,"* by Scott Bourne and David Middleton. In addition, she is working on a photo book documenting the beauty and strength of wolves. Carolyn also enjoys teaching, writing, and speaking about photography. She is a regular leader of photography workshops including for her own company, Vivid Wildlife Workshops; a moderator and columnist for www.Naturescapes.net (an online resource for nature photographers); and on the Advisory Council for the Picture Licensing Universal System (PLUS) (www.useplus.org), a worldwide coalition to define and standardize the core aspects of image licensing and its management.

Education and Honors: Carolyn graduated from Emory University School of Law with a Juris Doctor. She earned an American Jurisprudence Award for Legal Writing, Research and Advocacy and was awarded second place in the Nathan Burkham Legal Writing Competition on Copyright. She was the President of the Sports and Entertainment Law Society, Executive Candidacy Editor for the Emory Bankruptcy Developments Journal, and was selected the "most outstanding female law student."

Carolyn also graduated from Tennessee Technological University with a Masters of Business Administration degree and a Bachelor's of Science degree in music. She was a member of Omicron Delta Kappa (national leadership honor society), was designated an Outstanding Young Woman of America, and was awarded a four-year music scholarship.

Areas of Practice: Carolyn's practice covers all of the areas of concern to photographers—intellectual property law, including copyright and trademark law;

privacy law, including rights of privacy and rights of publicity; business and commercial law, including contracts; and commercial and tort litigation.

Professional Associations and Memberships: Carolyn is a member of the American Bar Association, North American Nature Photographers Association, American Society of Media Photographers, Editorial Photographers, Women in Photography International (Charter Member), and Picture Licensing Universal System (PLUS) (Advisory Council).

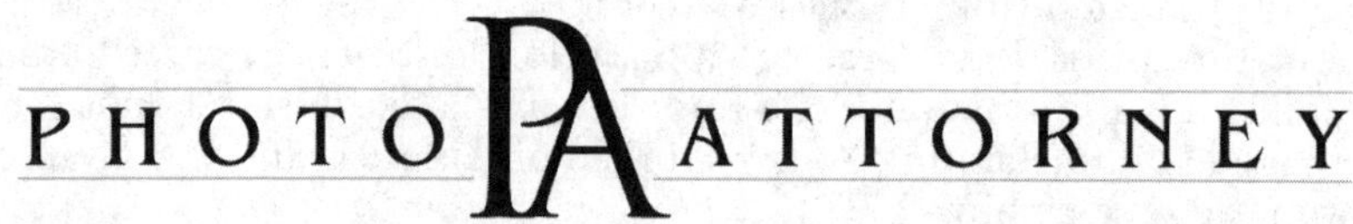

Photographer's Legal Guide

Need a Speaker?

Carolyn E. Wright, Esq., also is available as a speaker.

Contact her at:

Law Office of Carolyn E. Wright, LLC
2107 N. Decatur Road #117
Decatur, GA 30033
phone 678.592.8025
carolyn@photoattorney.com
www.photoattorney.com

Topics to be covered may be customized to include:

- Copyright Basics
    - What it is
    - Notice
    - Who owns it
    - Duration
    - Transferring your Copyright
- Rights of the Copyright Owner
- Protecting Your Copyrights
    - Registering your copyrights
    - How to register:
- Unpublished images
- Published images
    - Strategies
    - What is protected
    - What is not protected
- Prosecuting Your Copyrights
    - Remedies
- Demand Letters
- Digital Millennium Copyright Act
- Lawsuits
- Statute of Limitations
    - Practical techniques
- Licensing Your Photography
- Pricing Your Photography
- Rights of Photographers
- Rights of Privacy/Publicity
    - Model Releases
    - Tips for model releases
- Property Releases
    - Buildings
    - Other property

Book Order Form

Use this form to order additional copies of this book (USA residents only, please). Send the form with your payment to:

Law Office of Carolyn E. Wright, LLC
2107 N. Decatur Road #117
Decatur, GA 30033

Make your checks or money order payable to the Law Office of Carolyn E. Wright, LLC.

Please send me _______ copies of the Photographer's Legal Guide.

Enclosed is $19.95 (plus $3.95 for handling and shipping to USA) per copy. Call 678-592-8025 or email carolyn@photoattorney.com for bulk discounts.

Name: ____

Address: ____

____

Phone: ____

Email: ____

Index

corporation 3—6
court 2, 9, 25—26, 31—33, 43—44, 61, 67—73, 77—78, 80—81, 84, 89—90, 98
CPA. *See* accountant
creditor 4, 14
creditors 2—3, 5—6, 13—14
credit cards 7, 33—34
customs 22, 29, 96—98,

D

damages 9, 29—30, 37, 48, 51, 56, 59, 66, 70—71, 78, 80—85, 89
DBA. *See* doing business as
deductible 1, 17—19, 38—39
delivery memo 65, 83—85
deposit 51—58, 79—82
derivative work 43, 49, 53—54, 64, 76
Digital Millennium Copyright Act 67—69
disclaimer 78
doing business as 1, 4
domain 10, 48—50, 59, 87—89
dunning letter 31

E

editorial 53, 64, 88—91
EIN 6, 20
email 11—12, 34, 54, 75, 78—79
employees 4, 6, 20—21, 39, 49
employer identification number 6
equipment 7, 11, 17—18, 29, 34, 38—39, 41, 72, 96
estate planning 72
estimate 22—23
exclusive rights 42, 45, 51
expenses 1, 14—25, 33, 80—82

F

fair use 43—44, 93, 98
false light 87
FICA 20
fictitious name 1, 4, 6, 10
First Amendment 87—89, 97
foreign 8, 48, 63, 92—93
Form CA 60
Form PA 59
Form TX 59
Form VA 51

money orders 35
music 59, 62, 65, 91

N

national parks 94—95
non-exclusive 45

P

partnership 2—6, 37
Patent and Trademark Office 8
PayPal 34—35
personal assets 2—6, 37
photo credit 46, 67
Picture Licensing Universal System. *See* PLUS
PLUS 47
portrait 4, 7, 13, 29—30, 37, 46, 89
pricing 12
privacy rights 87
property 2—3, 7, 14, 18—20, 23, 26—27, 33, 37, 41, 43, 50, 65, 72—73, 76, 82—85,
    93—96
PTO. *See* Patent and Trademark Office
publication 17, 30, 51, 53—54, 57—58, 79, 89, 93
public domain 48—50, 59
published 30, 42, 48, 50, 53—64, 71—73, 87—93

R

register 1, 4—5, 8, 10, 51—54, 57—61, 64—65, 71—73, 76
registering 8, 10, 18, 50—56, 59—63, 68
registration 3, 7—10, 51—64, 71, 96
release 26—27, 81—85, 88—94
retainer 24, 30, 79—80
revision 60—61
right of privacy 87
right of publicity 87—90

S

sales tax 7, 15, 22—23
Schedule A 19
Schedule C 1, 19
Secretary of State 3, 5—6
Securities and Exchange Commission 4
servicemark. *See* trademark
SESAC 62

social security number 2, 20
sole proprietorship 1—2, 4, 37
SSN. *See* social security number
standing 26, 87
statute of frauds 77
statute of limitations 72
statutory damages 51, 56, 59, 71
subcontractor 20—21
sue 10, 26—27, 32, 68—69, 83, 93

T

tax 1—7, 11, 14—23, 73
tax ID number 6
trade 1—4, 10, 30, 41, 47, 65, 85, 87—88, 98
trademark 7—8, 10, 24—25, 93, 97—98
trade name 1—4, 10, 98
Transportation Security Administration. *See* TSA
TSA 95—96

U

U.S. Copyright Office. *See* Copyright Office
Uniform Commercial Code 13, 82
United States Patent and Trademark Office. *See* Patent and Trademark Office
unpublished 42, 51, 53—55, 57—58, 60, 63

W

warranty 85
website 8, 10, 11, 18—19, 35, 44, 50, 52—53, 57—59, 62, 67, 69, 72, 75—76, 90
wedding 29—30, 37, 46, 62, 76—78, 80—81, 89
work-for-hire 45—46, 52—54, 58

Z

zoning 7

Notes: